Penguinate!

Essays and Short Stories

Improve your creativity for a better life and a better world

By

Shad Engkilterra

Acknowledgements:

- Thank you to my Penguinators who support my family's artistic endeavors at www.patreon.com/penguinate. My wife makes amazing stuffed penguins that love to dress up.
    - Drue M. Scott
    - Patricia Burleigh
    - Mary Hawkins
    - Rachel O'Brien
    - Celia Wallis
- Thank you to the University of Malta and the Edward de Bono Institute for more than two years of creativity education.
- Thank you to the Walt Disney World College Program for the creativity course and the amazing experience that went with it.
- Thank you to my wife for allowing me to write as much as I can for as long as I can. Love you, honey!

Table of Contents

Creativity is active. It is dynamic. It is aggressive. If you aren't ready to work at your creativity, put this book down. There are no short cuts. There are no quick fixes. You won't have all the skills you need to create everything you want immediately. If you want to be a great painter, you're going to have to paint. If you want to be a great writer, you're going to have to write. If you want to be a great scientist, you're going to have to, uh, science.

Whatever you choose, to do it at the highest level, you need to be able to engage your creative mind. The dancing traffic cop and the Olympic hurdler were both engaging their creative selves in positions where everyone else is ruled by habit or decorum. Frank Lloyd Wright engaged his creative mind in the name of architecture. Steve Jobs and Bill Gates expressed their creativity through computers. They found satisfaction in their jobs and their lives because of their creativity.

I am not saying you can use creativity in your job. Creativity scares people because it brings change. There are a lot of people who won't understand your drive to try new things. Instead, they're going to want to get through their day without any changes. They don't want to think or take responsibility for not making things better. There are some jobs where creativity is unwelcome because the cost of failure or a mistake is so high.

I am saying that you can use creativity in your own life to bring you more... more joy, more happiness, and more fulfillment. It won't be easy. People won't always accept your particular creativity, but the important part is that you express, in a positive way, who you are. Be a builder, use your creativity and take the road less traveled. In other words, dance where you are and have fun.

If you got this as an eBook, be sure to keep a pen or pencil and some paper nearby. You have to practice your creativity if you want to get better at it. Regular book readers will have a few black pages throughout the book to do some writing or drawing. Be sure to share your results with "#penguinate" on your favorite social media.

What Is Penguinating?

Not all creativity is positive. Many people have used their creativity to help make things worse in the world. Advertisers knowingly hawking products that are harmful to their customers. Propaganda and lies told to win at all costs and make other people feel inferior. Even the successful robbing of a bank will take some sort of creativity as the bank robber has to overcome certain security measures. These are among the bad uses of the creative power of the human mind.

Penguinating focuses on the positive power of creativity. It attempts to consider how the results of the creative project will be used. Penguinators strive for beauty and truth. Creativity should be used for its powers to buildup, to create. Focusing your own creative powers to add something powerfully good to your life will not only improve your outlook, but it will also spill over into the lives of those you touch.

Create something and you'll feel good about it a lot longer than you'll feel good about destroying something. The reason why trolls proliferate on the Internet is because destruction eats itself. The more a person is able to tear apart, the more he or she needs to tear apart. Like a drug habit, it's never enough, and it infects others with its persistence and presence. Penguinating looks to the creative force that is in all of us to overcome the other side of the coin, the part of us that wants to destroy because we're not good at creating, because we feel powerless, because there is something primal in choosing to do the easy thing. Destruction is easy; creation never is.

Look to your better self and help others find their better selves. A person who is creative gives power to those around him or her to be creative, too. Become a Penguinator and help people move forward.

Ch 1: Believe You Can

Peter Pan said that if you wanted to fly you had to have three things: Faith, trust and pixie dust. Those three things are really all the same. Belief in yourself. Belief that you are creative and that you can become more creative are the first steps to becoming more creative. Have faith in yourself, trust that your mind, body and spirit will join in the creative effort, and the pixie dust will come. You can fly!

The following lessons are designed to help you find your creativity in the past and to build on them for the future. Join us as we explore creative aspects that are universal and individual.

A: Everyone Is Creative!

Everyone has the ability to be creative. If you think back to your childhood, you were creative. You sang, you danced, you held tea parties with your stuffed animals, you played cops and robbers or hot lava monster or cartoon tag, or any other game that didn't really follow the rules. The simple (and possibly passé) argument about a bullet, bulletproof vest, bullet proof vest piercing bullet, double bullet proof vest, laser, mirror repulsing laser during any of the shooting games that you played is evidence of creativity. If you had an imaginary friend, made up stories with your action figures or dolls or to explain things you couldn't understand, you were being creative. If you read a book, you were exercising your imagination and becoming more creative.

The problem is that society frowns on creativity because, on the whole, humans fear change and creativity brings change. It takes two or more old things and combines them into something new. That simple act is scary because new is different. It is unknown. It breaks the status quo, but as Dr. Horrible knows, the status is so not quo.

People who insist on being creative face a tough road as others put down the creative efforts of singing, dancing and art. Instead of learning how to think and change and embrace who they are, children are increasingly put in organized sports where conformity and following rules are valued. Both creativity and conformity are valuable in their place, and it is important that children learn to be creative and to know when to follow the rules.

In a society that values end results over process where the ends justify the means, the simple act of creation gets trodden into the mud, left to wallow as we give over to ideas that make us unhappy. It is important to recognize that you do not have to be the best at something for it to bring you joy. If people tell you that you are a terrible singer, sing anyway. If people say you can't dance, dance anyway. If someone ever told you that you couldn't draw, draw anyway. If it brings you happiness, grab onto it and do it. Be who you are, and love your life. Don't let others rain on it and drain it of the color you want to have in it.

Creation is an act of love. When you create, you can feel yourself fulfilling who you are supposed to become. You are self-actualizing. Allow yourself to embrace the power of creation dedicate yourself to doing something, anything creative. The list is long – writing, painting, drawing with crayons, dancing, cooking... Find something you enjoy doing and make it an art. Everyone can be creative. It just takes a little time and dedication.

Be active: If you are having trouble freeing yourself, find some children between the ages of two and eight to play with, preferably your own or your nieces and nephews or your friends' children. (Playing with stranger's children is really not a smart thing to do.) If you don't know any children to play with, think back to your own childhood and come up with one thing that you did that was creative. Was it a game you played? Was it a school project? Was it something you built at home? Go on your favorite social media platform and write it out: When I was a kid, I played Hot Lava Monster (or whatever was your creative thing)! Be sure to hashtag it (#penguinate).

B: The Skill of Creativity

The problem with talking about creativity as if it were separate from everything else is that it is not separate from everything else. Creativity only comes within a context of any sort. It is a metaskill that can be applied to any area of life. Businesses can be creative – Henry Ford's application of the assembly line was creative for its time. The creative arts include writing, painting, poetry, dance and sculpting, but creativity can be found in every part of life. Creativity is an ancillary asset that makes every job more fulfilling and enjoyable.

People might think that creativity is random, and while creative ideas can be had when randomness intervenes, creativity itself is a skill. Like everything that anyone wants to be good at, creativity takes discipline and commitment. Without these two qualities, the most gifted creative person in the world will only go as far as talent will take them. Michael Jordan was a gifted basketball player, but he added an intense training regimen and hours of practice to be the greatest player in the world. He could have gotten by on talent alone, but he was committed to his sport.

Discipline allows a person to set aside time every day to do something creative. It is the doing that allows the mind to free itself from the fear of failure and ridicule. It allows the mind to remember when creativity was a daily part of life. It allows the child to rise again and the adult to throw off the shackles of societal inhibitors. However, in order for there to be doing, there has to be discipline. People who want to get in shape get up early, exercise at lunch, or go to the gym after work even on days when they don't feel like it. People who want to be creative make time to do so. They stand in front of a canvas or a blank word document and start doing something even if they don't feel like it.

Creativity requires commitment because even if the creative effort succeeds, it is likely that the creator will be ridiculed. When someone invents something new, inevitably the naysayers come out and try to squash it. Critics make their money by tearing down what others have built, and they are often seen as intelligent for doing so. Creativity brings into being something new and unknown. It is scary, and quite often, the creative effort will fail. The creator needs to have the commitment to keep on creating. Great baseball players fail more than 60 percent of the time at the plate. Michael Jordan hit fewer than half of his shots. It is commitment that keeps the player in the game even when the game isn't going his or her way.

Be Active: Everyone can be creative. You've just got to make the commitment. Get a calendar. Choose a creative activity. Mark the time on your calendar when you're going to do this creative activity. Thirty minutes or more every day for the next two weeks. When you're done, tell the world how you succeeded in fulfilling your commitment (use "#penguinate") and set up your next commitment. Go out and do something to make the world happier through your creative efforts.

"When I was a child, I spake as a child, I understood as a child, I thought as a child: but when I became a man, I put away childish things." – King James Bible, 1 Corinthians 13:11

The arrogance of adults and growing up is in the belief that age changes people a great deal. The pervading theory in the Victorian era was that children were just little adults; however, no era has actually realized that just the opposite is true. Adults are just old children. Until society learns this, we will continue to stumble when trying to deal with each other.

Adults may have some theoretical advantages over children: better emotional control, different ways to learn new behaviors and more freedom. While grown-ups continue to delude themselves about these supposed advantages, the truth is that every adult is just a child with more worry, more responsibility, more pent up emotions and less fun.

"That's the real trouble with the world, too many people grow up." – Walt Disney

The unfortunate conversion to adulthood happens all through school as children go through the growing up process. Rather than learn how to be free thinkers, they are taught to conform, to be boring and to become less creative. In short, children go from being individuals to becoming a part of a group collective that will continue to support an ultimately unsustainable economic system. They will learn to fear and hate others while resenting the help given to those people who need it, especially when they have felt the same oppression and haven't received help when they needed it.

In every job that must be done, there is an element of fun. You find the fun, and SNAP! The job's a game. – Mary Poppins

Adults can regain their child-like qualities, and it can start with the right training. In every culture, children learn through play. It is only in later years that they are required to sit quietly and learn through lectures, PowerPoint presentations and textbooks. While people may be able to learn this way, they will retain very little of the information they are taught. Turning learning into an opportunity to play and have fun will result in a better overall command of the information to be learned.

Creativity is the ability to know how to play, to think outside the box and to apply logic and also imagination... Play more... Have a playful attitude... These things make you creative. – Tony Dyson

---

Be Active: Adults need to play. Find an empty playground, run on an empty field, or find a gaming group in your area (try your local comic book shop for suggestions). Go out and be childlike once more. Play. Then tell us about what you did on social media (#penguinate).

It's difficult for people to get a handle on what creativity is exactly. The American Psychological Association has been trying to define it officially since 1950. It always seems to have the quality of "we know what it is when we see it." Most often the process gets described in 4 or more steps and sometimes, someone will mention that these steps are recursive or non-consecutive. Whatever creativity is, there are many things that can stand in as a metaphor or a simile for it and for what the people who practice it should be like.

A: Pizza and Creativity

I really like vegetable topped pizza – the kind with red and green peppers, 5 kinds of cheese, spinach, onions, extra garlic, and maybe some artichoke hearts, feta, even olives and mushrooms if they have to be there. While there are several reasons for this, like vegetables are better for the environment and healthier than meat is, especially in the quantities that Americans eat meat, it is possible that the biggest reason why I like my pizza topped with vegetables is the flavor and texture mix that comes with those toppings.

Grease and Fat

Pizzas that have only one or two toppings cannot provide the flavor experience of a pizza with several kinds of toppings. While pepperoni pizza is good, especially when the pepperoni is crispy, it only allows the person eating it to experience the flavor of pepperoni, crust and cheese. Each bite is a variation on a theme with the amounts of pepperoni, crust and cheese varying, but no additional tastes coming into play. Meat also tends to overpower vegetables when they are mixed. The grease swarms and kills the flavor of fresh vegetables though onions are a notable exception to this phenomenon.

Different Taste Every Bite

With a cornucopia of vegetables on top of the pizza, every bite is different. One may be flavored by onions and green peppers, the next by spinach and a third by red peppers and olives. The combinations are endless (well, for at least as long as there is pizza left).

Pizza and Creativity

Relating the two types of pizza to creativity, pepperoni is the expert doing his or her job without ever questioning the status quo. This works fine in many jobs where it is important that the expert follow certain procedures. You don't want an airplane mechanic to start getting creative while he or she is maintaining a 747.

The different experiences that come with the vegetable pizza are like the experiences that help fuel creativity. The more varied the experiences, the more likely that someone who is creative will be able to find the creativity at the intersection. To be creative, people have to do different things and exercise their creative muscle. Creativity, much like a good vegetable covered pizza, adds more flavor to life.

Be Active: Go out, order a pizza you ordinarily wouldn't, and experience it. Let it cool off before you bite into. Smell it. See if you can identify each smell form the different ingredients. Does it smell like garlic, onions, pepper, or does it smell like sausage, ham and pepperoni, or is it all of the above? Look at it. See how the grease interacts with the rest of the ingredients and where it pools on the serving container. Once it's cooled, pick it up, see where the weight gets distributed in your hand and feel how it bends or doesn't. Then take a bite. If you burn the roof of your mouth, drink some cool water and wait a little longer. Then experience the flavors with each bite. Feel the texture every time you chew. Spend time experiencing your pizza and thinking deeply about it. Don't forget the selfie with "#penguinate" and your observations on your favorite social media.

B: The Four Horsemen of Creativity

Creativity leads to change. Since some people treat change like it's the end of the world, the Four Horsemen of Creativity are here to herald change is coming. If you wish to avoid change, you can try to avoid these harbingers of it. For your safety and education, I present descriptions of the Four Horsemen. Do not let them trample your status quo.

Horsing Around

The most basic form of creativity comes from play. Children learn about their world and process information through play. When people horse around, they are engaging in dangerous activities that may lead to the use of the imagination. Imagination leads to creative thinking. The best thing you can do to prevent the use of imagination is turn on the TV, play video games and hide all of the books. Make sure not to interact with others for any amount of time longer than it takes to complete a transaction. Joking is strictly prohibited.

Horsefeathers

When Horsing Around is present, Horsefeathers is nearby. The purveyor of all nonsense, this horseman allows humor to flourish and imagination to fly. It is only through nonsense that sense can be made, especially in creative arenas. The crazy idea may be the one that leads to the breakthrough for big change. Do not allow nonsense to take over your conversations, and avoid anything written by Lewis Carroll.

Horse of Another Color

Creativity happens at the intersection. When one person is talking about something and another person brings in an entirely different subject, you can bet that the Horse of Another Color has been there. These two people may be able to take the two ideas and combine them into something new – that is what creative people do. The combination of two ideas into something new is at the core of all creative activities and leads to change quickly. That makes this horseman the most dangerous of them all.

Horse Sense

There are people who are super-creative, but they never accomplish anything. This is because they lack Horse Sense. In order for creativity to create any kind of change, it must be turned into something tangible and useful. Even the most creative person with a million ideas will not create any sort of change unless those ideas are put into action. Ideas need to be communicated in a way that other people will understand and accept them. Once that happens, the apocalypse of change will come, and it will be heralded by the stamping hooves of the four Horsemen.

Be Active: Make a joke. Engage in nonsense. Learn something new. Read a fiction book; "Alice in Wonderland," for example. Talk with another person about an idea or a problem that needs a creative solution. Create something and share it on social media with "#penguinate."

C: The Cockroaches of Creativity

Artists, dreamers and innovators like to think of creativity as a beautiful thing. However, creation is difficult, being a creator is hard work, and creativity, in its many forms, is treated as if it were a cockroach. It is to be feared and exterminated before it affects any type of change for good or ill.

Creativity is hard to kill. People who suppress their creative desires often end up with psychological issues. Some just become very unpleasant to be around. They are grouchy and unable to take the appropriate steps to self-actualization. Creativity will find a way, and it will just keep coming back.

Creativity contaminates other people. Even those who profess they are not creative, when surrounded by coworkers or friends who are, become more creative. When creatives live or work in a place where others are creative, they become even more creative.

Creativity is scary. Being creative means bringing change to the world. Change is scary. Most people would rather live comfortably than deal with change. Creativity will make them uncomfortable.

Creativity is rarely tolerated, so it has to be done in the dark. In the basement, in the shed, in the garage... There are a lot of places where people can be creative – out in the real world isn't one of those places. Fortunately, creativity can thrive in the dark because it is acceptable there. It also needs to be exposed to the light to find out what it really is.

Creativity often gets stomped on, but it cannot be stomped out. Let us embrace and become the cockroaches of creativity. We will be hard to kill. We might be ugly. We might have to practice our creative powers in the dark. But we will keep coming back. Every incarnation will be stronger than the one before, and some of us will fly.

Be Active: Finish your creative project and show it to the world. Don't forget to mark it with "#penguinate." If you get negative comments, it's okay. You'll be stronger for the next unveiling.

Ch. 3: Creativity and Emotions

Amidst all of the turmoil of the world, people have found solace in the power to create. Even while he was in a Russian POW camp during World War II, Emil "Elwa" Waas painted with the materials that he had. Blood and grass were among the paints, and fingernails and hair served as brushes. Ancient man painted on the walls of caves. Creativity has been used to cope with horrific conditions both real and imagined since man could create. Stories were told to pass the time and pass down history and tribal information. Dances were created to make it rain and honor the gods. Even David found a secret chord. You can harness your creativity to help you cope with your emotions and what is most difficult to deal with in the world.

When the world looks bleak and you're just too tired,
Go to your place, light a creative fire,
And build something up with your own two hands
Or find the words to understand.

When the world's problems are immense and you feel small,
When you watch the news ad can't deal at all,
Go to your place and exercise your creative power
For 10 minutes or several hours.

Whether it is a Picasso or something LOL,
The product of your creation isn't the goal.
It's the creative process, the journey, you seek
To explore, expose, practice and tweak.

The more you do, the more you'll see,
You have the power to change the world, your life, the way to be.
It just lays dormant like a dragon of yore
Waiting for you to awaken and release its roar.

Strength, vitality, peace and more
Are within your grasp and within your core.
You just need some time and space and silent repose,
A moment to build, to compose.

Seek this power and you will find.
Peace, love and joy aren't just in the mind.

Be active: Write your own poem to express how you feel about creativity and creation. Share it using "#penguinate."

B: A Salve against Destruction

As the world beats the drums of war, it is time for the ordinary citizen to do what he or she best can to balance out the destruction that war brings. Destruction is easy. The slide of a knife and the pull of a trigger can end a life that took years to create. The dropping of a bomb can level buildings and destroy centuries old history. One false word and trust is doomed. Humans engage in destruction as they rage against the machine, riot for justice and step across the border into another country. Destruction comes as easy to people as eating, cursing and consumption.

People have a greater side, but it takes a little more work. People are naturally creative. It is the builder, the painter, the author who must now take up their tools to make the world a better place. Each person can make something, and in that act of creation, every man, woman and child shows our baser nature that people will not be cowed by the warmongers.

While Russia invades the Ukraine, ISIL/ISIS/IS is cutting off the heads of journalists and killing people and the news focuses on every wrong and terrible thing that our nation's leaders are doing, it is natural to feel angry and impotent. However, people should not allow that anger, even if it is righteous, to become who they are. By rolling that anger and those feelings into an act of creation, people are living up to their best selves. For anyone who believes that people are children of God, the ability to be creative is easy to see. After all, His talent to make things is surpassed by none, His children have the same talent.

Even those who do not believe that people are the children of God can look back on their own childhoods to find that they were once creative, and what a person once was, he or she can be again. Israeli Ronny Edry can be a guide in the face of state, militant and terrorist aggression. A graphic designer whose movement went viral and engaged the world in acts of solidarity and peace, Edry took his creativity and found a way to express his personal views. Israel Loves Iran resulted in a reciprocal movement in Iran, where people risked their loves to talk about their love for Israelis.

Most people want the same things in life – food, safety, family, friends – there are a few who substitute the horrors of war to feel powerful, and those few drag the rest of the world into their madness. The average person stands impotent while these forces rage, but he or she has one sure way to exercise his or her own personal power. The power of creativity can help ease the pain of destruction and the feelings that come with the evening news.

Be Active: Build something, paint something, draw something, write something. It doesn't matter what it is, just use your creativity to build a little beauty and help heal the destruction of the world. Share it if you want (#penguinate).

C: 4 Steps to Coping with Fear, Loss, and Sadness

With politics and events being what they are, there is a pretty good chance that you are feeling powerless to do anything to change the world for the better. You probably also feel frustrated, sad and angry. Maybe you have reached the apathetic stage. After all, even babies and puppies are affected by injustice. If they can sense it without having words for it, it must be more pronounced for those who can examine situations and explain them.

If you are feeling this way now, imagine how you will feel the next time there is a mass killing of people, or a cop shoots a seemingly helpless man who is complying, or someone shoots a cop, or someone accidentally shoots his mother or his son – BECAUSE IT WILL HAPPEN AGAIN. Imagine how you will feel after the next election – because no matter who wins, everyone making less than a million dollars loses.

If you like feeling these emotions, and it is clear that there are plenty of people who thrive on tragedy so you're not alone, then stop reading now and go back to watching FOX "News" or MSNBC. However, if you want to change the way you feel and have a way to cope with the unthinkable events that have become all too common, follow these four steps:

1. **Set up a space** – Find a place where you can be alone or with friends. Make that space conducive to creating. The space should have all of the tools you need for your particular brand of creativity. Pen, paper, clay, paints, Legos... Whatever it is that you find comforting. The space will also need rules. No judging, no interrupting the creative process, no cell phones, no PokemonGo. This space is for you to practice creativity. That also means that there is no failure. If you're in this space doing something creative, you have already succeeded.

2. **Invite friends and family** – Some creative activities are better when shared. This will also help you build relationships and create a support network. Ideas generally get better when there is someone around to work with. Again, the rule is "no judging." "Yes, if..." is the best phrase to use here.

3. **CREATE!** You are a human being. Your most powerful weapon against drifting into inhumanness is the ability to create. It doesn't matter if you create something brilliant or a lump of clay that vaguely looks like mashed potatoes if seen from far away. What matters is that you are releasing your most personal and strongest drive, a drive that the school system and capitalism have tried to eliminate from the human race. As the world spins towards entropy, creating is the only way that individuals can fight against the destruction. The world needs you to create beauty, love, relationships, art and joy. Follow the Carpenters lead and don't worry if it's not good enough for anyone else. It is good enough for you.

4. **Share your creation** – God knows there's enough crap on social media, adding your creation will give others the opportunity to explore their abilities to create. Sharing is the hardest thing to do, and you may have people in your network who will laugh at or ridicule you. Let them laugh, laughing is good. Put the block on those who would ridicule you, you don't need that negativity in your life. Make sure to hashtag it with #penguinate.

You might not be able to go to war against ISIS/ISIL/IS, or whoever the enemy is this month, but you can go to war against their ideals. While they destroy the history of mankind, you can rebuild it with your creativity. (Or didn't you realize that these terrorists are offended by "graven" and "pagan" images.)

Fight terrorist ideals, fight boredom, fight apathy, and fight powerlessness. Using the power of creativity, you can become your own superhero. You just have to commit to doing it and then unleash your strength.

Be Active: Follow the four steps. Share photos of your work station, you and your friends, and your creations! Always #penguinate.

Ch 4: The Evolution of an Idea

Creativity starts with an idea. That idea may jump up at you and need to be manifested immediately, or it may take years to gestate and become a full-fledged creative project. Having ideas is one thing; bringing it to life is another. Ideas must be captured, even if they don't seem like they are useful now.

A: The Birth of Disneyland

On Daddy Sundays, Walt Disney would take his girls to Griffith Park, sit on a bench and eat peanuts while he watched Diane and Sharon ride the merry-go-round. He thought there had to be something better. There had to be a place where parents and children could enjoy doing things together. There had to be a place where adults could play with the kids.

The idea for Disneyland was born! Sort of.

Walt would get letters from children who wanted to meet Mickey Mouse. They would ask if they could come to the studio, and he thought that a studio tour would be a bit boring for children. So, he dreamed up an amusement park across the road from the studio where kids could go and meet Mickey Mouse. Soon his plan for the acreage across the road was too large, he was going to need more land.

The idea for Disneyland was born! At least it was closer.

Walt needed to get money for his new theme park, something that had never been built before. His wife, Lilly asked him why he would want to own a dirty amusement park; he said that was the point, his wouldn't be. She wasn't the only one who had reservations about the park. His brother Roy was going to help Walt's dream come true and had a meeting with some bankers. Roy told Walt that he needed something to show the bankers because they wouldn't get what Walt was trying to do just from a description. It was Friday. Roy was meeting with the bankers on Monday.

The Lost Weekend

Walt called in Herb Ryman and told him about Disneyland. Ryman asked Walt to see the plans, and Walt told Ryman that Ryman was going to draw them. Ryman blanched and would only do it on the condition that Walt stayed with him the entire weekend. The deal was struck; Ryman had the drawing ready for Roy before the meeting with the bankers.

And the idea for Disneyland was born! Finally... Mostly.

The problem with choosing an exact date for the idea of Disneyland is that there is no exact date. Walt Disney was a man who let ideas germinate, he collected experiences and things that fascinated him, he looked at problems and tried to find solutions, and he never really let time stand in his way. He had deadlines that he had to meet, but he also knew he had to do everything the best way possible. He would scrap entire storylines until the creative people could get it right. He would scrap thousands of dollars' worth of animation to make a scene better. He would sit on ideas until he had the right solution to make what he wanted happen.

Even with the Herb Ryman drawing, Walt's idea wasn't complete. In fact, Disneyland was the answer to several of Walt's problems. Walt knew that once a movie was made, it was done; he wanted to be able to tweak them but couldn't.

Disneyland gave Walt something he could change for the better as often as he wanted.

Disneyland will never be done as long as there is imagination left in the world. We can point to July 17, 1955 as the date that the park was officially open, but even this date is a little artificial since guests enjoyed Walt and Lilly's anniversary on the Mark Twain in the park before the public was let in. Some would point to July 18 as the first day the park was open to the public officially.

As the park continues to evolve with the opening of Star Wars: Galaxy's End, the question of when an idea is truly born may be a moot point. After all, any idea that is made into something will have to evolve with time or it will cease to exist. Fortunately, Walt knew that and he planned for Disneyland to continue changing.

Be Active: Draw up your own theme park. Don't worry if you can't build it, yet, just put in all the awesome stuff you want to see in a theme park. Then change something about it. Be sure to share it with "#penguinate."

B: Critical Failure for Success

"Champions" is a generic superhero game that allows players to make superheroes. You choose your characters power, spend a certain amount of points to get those powers and upgrade the powers as the game progresses.

One of the things that makes role-playing games like life is the idea of random chance. Because every good role-playing game has rules and dice so that the Game Master (GM), the person who runs or coordinates the story/game, can't just make up the story (even though GMs often do this regardless of the roll), there is an amount of random chance to every risky interaction. Players can't just charm non-player characters as played by the GM and expect it to work every time. No matter how good an archer is he or she would not hit the target every time. Dice help to make the randomness neutral and unexpected.

What every player hopes to roll is a critical success. In D&D, that means rolling a 20 on a 20-sided die. It means that the action succeeded more than anyone could have thought. Not only did the archer hit the target, but he split his opponent's arrow while it was still in the air and still hit the spot dead on. Everything just goes better with a critical success – potions become more effective, enemies give up or lose limbs, and thieves are extra sneaky.

What no player wants, unless an awesome GM is involved, is a critical failure. This is akin to falling on your sword on accident, having your bow break as you draw it back or tripping and spraining an ankle. (Lots of characters in horror films must make a critical failure rolls as the monsters are chasing them through the woods).

In "Champions," I had character named Dioxin. She got her calcium-based powers because she drank so much milk directly from the carton. (This was back during the huge milk carton/dioxin scare.) She could suck the calcium from people's bones; she could also heal the people by replacing the calcium. I don't remember what she wanted to do at the time I made the roll but it was a critical failure.

The GM of the game immediately said that instead of accomplishing whatever it was, Dioxin emitted an explosion of calcium chunks all around her. This gave me, the player, an opportunity to further develop her skills as she tried to control the explosion and make it something useful the next time. It also gave my character more depth. (Plus, the GM described it so awesomely and fluidly that he seemed to have planned for it.)

In Dioxin's case, it wasn't her successes that made her more interesting but her failures. I suspect that the most interesting people in the world are the ones who have overcome failures to meet success.

Be Active: Which failure has most enhanced your life? Share (#penguinate).

Ch 5: The Creative Personality

Csikszentmihalyi claimed ten characteristics that, while seemingly the opposite of each other, were present in creative individuals:

- Introvert/extrovert
- High energy/often at rest
- Smart/naïve
- Playful/disciplined
- Fantasy/reality
- Humble/proud
- Rebellious/conservative
- Passionate/objective
- Psychologically androgynous
- Open and sensitive to suffering and enjoyment

Having parts of these characteristics would make one person diametrically opposed to him or herself if these traits are considered in their traditional sense and if people are supposed to be consistent.

The problem is that people are not consistent, and these traits can be expressed by people at different times depending on the circumstance. An introvert can go to a party and appear extroverted. Creative people typically need some form of human contact if they are going to be any good at what they do. However, once the creative person has started working, he or she may shut him or herself up for long periods of time.

Creatives may work maniacally on a project, but when it is finished, there may be a period of rest. Sometimes, the creative work appears to be rest to the outsider because the person is doing the work inside of his or her head. This takes concentration and requires a state where the person should not be interrupted even by simple movements of the body.

The real problem is that people are not consistent across the board or within the framework of their own beliefs and values. Someone who finds abortion abhorrent may be okay with letting poor children starve and the death penalty. Someone who claims that education is important may have never gone to school. A person who chooses coffee day after day could wake up one morning and choose tea.

"Foolish consistency is the hobgoblin of little minds," said Ralph Waldo Emerson. While corporations and consumers value consistency and people like the predictability that consistency brings with it, human beings themselves are, at the individual level, only consistent for as long as they are consistent. Being able to express a full range of traits is exactly what people should be able to do. There is no need to be labeled either smart or naïve when a person can be both. In fact, being both may be intrinsic to a person's ability to experience a full life.

Be Active: Give us a humble brag (#penguinate).

A: Creative Block from a Writer's POV

Here we are again – in front of a blank page with nothing to write. For a writer, this can be one of the most frustrating events in his or her career. The blank page and nary an idea in sight... It isn't really true that there isn't an idea in sight. Any good writer probably as a notebook full of ideas, about which he or she could write, but for whatever reason, none of those ideas are providing the creative spark that is the impetus for a good article, or at least one that is passable enough for the website.

There are several reasons why a writer might experience a block like this. The writer's emotional state, a lack of recent experiences, a lack of sleep, a lack of motivation, too much work and being on deadline are just a few.

The writer's emotional state can make or break his or her writing ability; the tricky part is knowing which emotions block writing altogether and which lend themselves to other types of writing. Writers who like to write criticism, sometimes, need to be angry to write something that sells. Some poets need to be in love to write poetry while others need to be falling out of love or experiencing some sort of internal strife. The hardest state to write in though is one of apathy.

Apathy is the idea that nothing I do matters, so why do anything. For those who are not familiar with the apathetic feeling, it helps to think about politics – how much does your one vote count? You should still do it, but will it make a difference? Writers who are working from an apathetic standpoint, probably aren't actually working. It is hard to write when what you write doesn't matter, or at least, feels like it doesn't matter. Of course, apathy spreads from the writing to the rest of life. If there appears to be no reason to write, the writer is probably going to stop. Why bleed on a page when you can keep your dullness to yourself? It's nice to be comfortably numb. Apathy often leads to a lack of motivation.

Having a reason to write makes all the difference when it comes to being able to continue to write. Inspiration can come from anywhere, but the writer has to be open to it, and that means finding the reason to put fingers to keyboard and start typing away. If you write for a loved one, write to pay the bills or write for another reason, you may find that your words will flow more freely. It is important, however, to choose the right motivation. If the loved one goes away or the writer can't pay the bills, he or she will become demotivated and find it difficult to write again. On the other hand, having someone, who can help open the writer up, will dramatically increase his or her productivity when it comes to generating new content.

Be Active: Share your reasons to be creative with the hashtag: #penguinate.

B: The Persistence of a Gamer

In "Edge of Tomorrow," Tom Cruise portrays Bill Cage an army officer who is demoted and gains the ability to reset time. He can only do so, however, by dying. The premise of living the same day over and over was more successfully and hilariously explored by Bill Murray's Phil Connors in "Groundhog Day," a film that seems to exist because every other holiday already had stories attached to them.

Both characters experience a sort of malaise as they are exploring their own personal time loops. Connors goes through doing all of the bad things possible and then trying to kill himself; nothing changes the fact that he is experiencing the same day over and over. Cage only gets one or two scenes where he is clearly not doing what he should be doing – one finds him drinking in a bar where his courage is questioned.

However, neither character ever learns helplessness. They both continue living without becoming truly inured in their own personal hells. Connors strives to become a better person, saving kids and learning the piano. He finally uses his time wisely and is released from the continual repetition of the day. Cage gets better at fighting and learns to become brave. His release comes at the hands of a blood transfusion, and it is not one that he covets.

Gamers are known for their persistence in doing the same thing over and over. In an overview of their behavior, they mash the same buttons again and again though the results are different on the screen, the actions are often the same. However, their most important trait is their ability to explore a world that they have conquered multiple times.

Gamers can play the same game over and over without ever quitting regardless how difficult the task or how much or little is left to find. They are the ones that find the hidden Easter eggs and worlds. While neither Cage nor Connors were gamers in their respective worlds, they exhibit the same kind of relentless persistence necessary to conquer a battlefield, a job, or a video game.

Be Active: Adopt a gamer's point of view for your creativity. Every rejection is just another obstacle, another barrier overcome, or another attempt at an Easter egg. Keep submitting your idea; keep practicing your creativity. Keep at it until to reach your goal. Share your rejections (#penguinate).

C: Living Life in the Face of Death

"The Fault in Our Stars" is one of those movies that gets people to think about life by using the imminent death of teenagers as the catalyst for the thought process. Like every other movie, book or thought on the process of living, the teens do not think about getting that dream job and working for the next 40 or 50 years to do what they want when they retire. They think about living right now. That is the key to life. Living in the moment and experiencing what life has to offer.

While it may be cliché to use a terminal illness to point out what is most important in life, there is a reason to do so. Everyone dies a little bit each day. Some people get up and die all at once; some do not get up at all, and many never see it coming. Yet, the specter of death rarely hangs over the person who is in good health. People do not like to think about death, so it takes a movie, the death of someone close or an actual personal brush with death to get someone to start thinking about what is really important in life.

A terminally ill teen or child is the perfect way to get that message across. Illnesses like cancer have the possibility of going into remission, so it is not a foregone conclusion that the character will die. Teens and children with terminal illnesses are portrayed as preternaturally intuitive, wise beyond their years and always in a fighting mood, except for those small moments of self-doubt that they rarely let others see. These traits may indeed be in every child who experiences a terminal illness though they are rare in the population at large.

Whether it is the closeness to death, the ordeal that they have to endure or another reason, these are also the traits that are required to move a story forward to the point about what life is. Those who know they are dying are also the ones who are living life. Those who ignore death also tend to ignore life. It is small wonder that people ignore both or embrace both because they are two sides of the same coin, and no one can touch one without touching the other.

"The Fault in Our Stars" proposes that the thing that matters most in life is not thousands of adoring fans, but just one person who loves another person deeply. That is all that matters. As the love develops between the reluctant Hazel Grace Lancaster and the amorous and persistent Augustus Waters, there is no discussion about what they could be or would be when they grew up because for them there is no growing up. They find each other and embrace the love that forms between them, even knowing that one of them will end up in pain because of the death of the other – reinforcing the idea that love is the most important thing in life.

Be Active: Live life. Stop hiding behind bills and grudges. Stop procrastinating. Go out right now, and do one thing you've always wanted to do. Experience it fully. Be there in the moment. Come back and tell us about it (#penguinate).

Ch 6: Get Back Your Power

While human ingenuity is at the heart of every advancement for people throughout millennia, life isn't built for creativity. It's well documented that schools, for the most part, try to quell the child's traits of imagination, curiosity, and creativity in an effort to bring order and quiet to the classroom. The workplace and the world after school is no different. However, the way you give up your power may be subtler than you realize. Too many choices and not enough faith in your own intuition and abilities play a role in keeping you from being more creative. It's time to get that power back.

A: Instinctive Archery for Empowerment

With the rise of tools like computers, GPS and Smartphones, humanity has also seen a rise in feelings of powerlessness. Personal empowerment doesn't come from having gadgets for every occasion; it comes from knowing that you have the strength and improvisational skills to meet those times when adversity rears its head and you are tested. You can only know that you have those skills if you practice them. Let them sit in a fallow field, and your skills will erode like a plow left to the elements.

"In ½ a mile, turn left. In 1/10 of a mile, turn left. Turn left at the next street. Turn left now. Recalculating... In 1/10 of a mile, turn left." A talking GPS is a great tool. However, when it is relied upon too heavily, it can erode a person's confidence in knowing where he or she is and how to get to or from an area. Knowing how to read a map is a skill. Knowing how to navigate using the sun and landmarks is a skill. Both of these skills empower the person who has them, especially when the electricity or power goes out or no satellites are available.

"25 + 34? Wait, let me use my calculator." Simply solving a math equation can be empowering. You are showing and using skills that give you the power to solve a problem, literally. This literal solving of a problem creates confidence in your abilities and capabilities. Pushing buttons is not a skill that creates the feeling of accomplishment necessary for greater self-belief.

The more technology and tools that you put between you and your skills, the less confident in your own skills you become. One place where this is easy to see is on the archery range. Someone trained in instinctive archery will pick up an unfamiliar bow without a sight, without a counterbalance, without even an arrow rest and be able to use that bow. Someone who is used to having a sight will ask how to aim, and someone who uses a counterbalance will end up throwing the bow on the ground forgetting that it has no counterbalance.

An archer that trains to trust that the body will work together with the mind to get the arrow to hit the target will only miss when he or she isn't fully aligned in purpose. It is this alignment and focus, and the confidence that it breeds, that becomes the archer's greatest weapons and greatest tools. The bird isn't afraid of the branch breaking, not because it has confidence in the branch but because it has confidence in its wings.

Be Active: Find an instinctive archery course near you. Take it. If there is no course, learn to read a map or solve math problems without a calculator or your phone. Share how you feel (#penguinate).

B: Choice, Happiness and Online Dating

According to Dan Slater (2013), one-third of America's 90 million singles are using online dating services to find relationships that range from one-night stands and cheating on their significant others to long term relationships and marriage. The internet offers daters seemingly unlimited choices in whom they date. Sites can be as general as Match.com, more discerning like eHarmony or as specific as JDate which caters to those who are looking to date someone who is Jewish either culturally or religiously.

According to Barry Schwartz (2004), western culture views choice as the ultimate expression of individual freedom. However, unbridled choice has some serious side effects for our culture in general and for relationships specifically, especially for those who try to maximize every decision. These maximizers are only satisfied if they have chosen the best available; unfortunately, with all of the choices available, there is no way to be sure that the choice a maximizer has made is truly the best choice.

When choice becomes so overwhelming, satisfaction with choices that are made go down, even when those choices were good. Opportunity costs, counterfactual imaginings, adaptation, and increased expectations add together to create dissatisfaction. Slater's (2013) assertion that the strength of relationships is based on satisfaction level, investment size and the quality of alternatives when considered in conjunction with Schwartz's (2004) theories on why more is less make it easy to see why, as Slater (2013) writes, 39 percent of people believe that marriage is becoming obsolete and both the age that people get married and the divorce rate are rising.

Opportunity costs are those things that we give up in order to enjoy something else. I can either go to dinner and a movie or go to a baseball game. Each situation involves good points and bad points. I can only choose one activity, and doing so involves losing out on some things. I may be trading the intimacy of a dinner and a movie for the excitement of a ball game.

Schwartz says that people's satisfaction levels decrease as they consider the trade-offs involved in making a choice. In fact, people are so averse to making trade-offs, that if they can avoid making a decision that involves trade-offs, they will. The problem is that the trade-offs to be made do not exist between two or three products, but they exist amongst all of the options available. Not only am I comparing the trade-offs involved in a dinner and a movie versus going to a ball game, but I am also considering the trade-offs that come when I add other possible activities like a picnic in the park or a night at the theater.

Furthermore, Schwartz believes that trade-offs include all of the options that someone can imagine even when they do not exist. That means that someone in a relationship may become less satisfied with the relationship not only as he or she meets people who have qualities that the chosen significant other does not, but also as the person imagines someone who has all of the qualities that the significant other does not. Amy Webb (2013) talks about her experience in online dating and how she didn't want to accidentally miss out on the perfect man.

Counterfactual imaginings are the suppositions that one makes when describing a past that could never be. For example, if I had only gone out with AngelBaby23 instead of JuicyFruit12, I would have had a better time. The fact is that I went out with AngelBaby23, and I cannot change what has happened. Beyond that, what is conjured by the imagination is not necessarily what would have occurred. JuicyFruit12 may have turned out to be a psycho killer having a bad day, but that is probably not what I am going to imagine. These counterfactual imaginings add to the regret that the person feels about a decision that he or she has made.

Adaptation is the ability of people to create a state of normal around any situation, which can be a good thing when normal is less than optimal. For example, people who become quadriplegic, according to Schwartz (2004), are just as happy, after a period of adjustment, as people who haven't experienced such a dramatic change in life. They get used to their limitations and learn to enjoy the things they can do.

While adaptation is good in bad experiences, it can also decrease the enjoyment of good experiences. Schwartz (2004) illustrates this with the idea of great wine. If someone indulges in a great wine every night, the enjoyment of that wine lessens over time. If that same person, however, saves the great wines only for special times, it is sure to be more pleasing during those times because the person will not have gotten used to it. Expanding this idea to relationships, it is clear that even a great relationship can suffer as each person gets used to the other. Even getting flowers every day can become an expected experience that gets taken for granted when it is done and, as in the duet by Neil Diamond and Barbara Streisand (1978), becomes a point of contention when it isn't.

With online dating, there are increased expectations not only in who is available to date, but in how the relationship will progress. Slater (2013) believes that there is an expectation that the computer must know something that the daters don't, so that online dating shouldn't lead to just more dates, but that it should lead to better dates. Webb's (2013) experiences show that online dating does not necessarily lead to better dating, and both Slater and Webb point out that online dating sites do not necessarily want daters to be successful. The key to profit through online dating are good dates but not great ones, so that daters continue to use the online services.

Schwartz (2004) points out that when experiences do not meet expectations, people become disappointed. If eHarmony users expect that they will meet the perfect person through eHarmony, they will be disappointed. This disappointment can lead to depression and learned helplessness as the bad experiences pile up, and each will be bad because it doesn't live up to expectations.

The proliferation of online dating sites and the perceived ease with which one can engage in new relationships has led to less investment in relationships as a whole. According to Schwartz (2004), when someone is able to exchange an item after purchase, that person has less investment in that item. The same can be said of relationships. The more choice that people have and the easier a relationship is to find, the easier it becomes to jettison a relationship that just isn't going well.

Slater's (2013) says that strong relationships are based on satisfaction level, the amount of investment and the quality of alternatives. It is clear that the choices that online dating provides cause relationships to be shorter and less satisfying. Satisfaction goes down because of greater expectations, perceived opportunity costs that accumulate over time and counterfactual imaginings. Investment is less because it is easier to find another relationship than it has been in the past, and the perceived quality of the alternatives is greater because of the multitudes of choice.

This does not mean that online dating is entirely responsible for the unraveling of the social fabric. Slater (2013) and Schwartz (2004) also agree that choice gives people the feeling of being autonomous and those feelings can lead to greater psychological and physical health. Schwartz believes that as long as people are aware that too many choices can be detrimental, they can protect themselves. He suggests establishing self-limiting rules to make choices easier and committing to the choice once it has been made. As Slater (2013) says, "Any technology that helps people to find companionship, and not be alone, offline, is something to be thankful for."

Be Active: Go to the store with the largest cereal aisle in your area. Choose a cereal that you don't normally get. Share why you chose it and how you felt about the experience (#penguinate).

References:

Diamond, Neil, and Barbra Streisand. You Don't Bring Me Flowers. Columbia, 1978. CD.

Schwartz, Barry. The Paradox of Choice: Why More Is Less. New York: Ecco, 2004. Print.

Slater, Dan. Love in the Time of Algorithms: What Technology Does to Meeting and Mating. New York: Current, 2013. Print.

Webb, Amy. Data, a Love Story: How I Gamed Online Dating to Meet My Match. N.p.: Penguin Group (USA) Incorporated, 2013. Print.

C: Structuring Your Life for Creativity

The "Structuring Your Life to Support Creativity" panel at Salt Lake Comic Con 2014 started with a declaration: "We all have lives full of things." We need "more room for the things we love and less room for the things we don't." Participants Sandra Tayler, Shannen Camp, Julie Wright, Sarah E. Seeley and Scott William Taylor talked about how to make life better for creative pursuits. The most important thing is a support network.

"My biggest fan is my wife, and she wants me to keep writing," says Scott Taylor, without her it would next to impossible.

Sandra Tayler says that there are sometimes people in our lives that damage our creativity, and there are others, like children and dogs, who are obstacles.

"Time is precious," says Wright. "I never find time ever. I have to make time."

"Those distractions, you just have to work around them."

"It's nice to establish boundaries with loved ones," says Camp. "This is a job... so let's keep the time separate."

As for children, it is important to teach them to be competent. They can clean up their own messes.

Time to Write

"Carve out a time to do it," says Scott Taylor. "Write every day." Sometimes you can get writer's block, and that can kill you.

Sandra Tyler says that writing at the same time every day trains your brain.

Seeley says that the optimal time for her to write is between 2 a.m. and 5 a.m.

"I can be completely creative" because I am so tired that I don't care how bad it is, says Seeley.

As for setting up the time and place, Sandra Tayler recommends that you create a special physical space to create the writer's mindset. It can be as simple as opening a laptop. It is just a matter of training the brain by being consistent with the actions that lead to writing.

"You can learn this. You can train your brain. Keyboard's open. Now it's time to write," says Tayler.

Finding 15 minutes a day works for Wright. It only takes 250 words to make a page.

"Pick some things that you are supposed to do and skip them," says Tayler, as way of carving out time.

Camp finds it is also important to be able to give yourself a break as long as you don't get into the habit of not writing. Wright agreed.

"You need to fill your creative well," says Wright. "Know what inspires you."

Exercise, eating right and socializing are important to creativity for Seeley.

"Don't give up on getting back to your creativity," says Seeley, if someone has to take extended time off due to family emergency or prolonged illness.

Scott Taylor advises people to not compare themselves to others.

Creativity inspirations

- Arts
- Video Games
- Doing chores
- Spending time with people
- Yardwork
- Community theater – "It requires you to work with other people," says Scott Taylor. "Any time you are with creative people, it can charge you."

Sandra Tayler recommends just getting out of the house and finding new stimuli. Carry a notebook and write it down when it comes. You can even use your phone. Train your brain to remember what's important. Tell your brain it is important and then follow up on it.

"As creative people, in general, we are hares," says Sandra Tayler. Sometimes it is more important to be the tortoise.

Wright recommends just filling up the blank page even if the writing is bad.

"You can fix stupid," says Wright. "You cannot fix a blank page."

"Anything you practice at, you get better at," says Sandra Tayler. Art is never finished; it is only abandoned.

"Fostering creativity is allowing mistakes to happen," says Scott Taylor.

"Stay determined. Balance that with other things in your life," says Seeley. "People are more important than your craft."

"Everyone is creative in a different way," says Camp.

Be Active: Find your way to be creative. Share (#penguinate).

"A lot of people in our industry haven't had very diverse experiences. They don't have enough dots to connect, and they end up with very linear solutions, without a broad perspective on the problem. The broader one's understanding of the human experience, the better designs we will have" – Steve Jobs, "Wired," February, 1996. "[Creative people] were able to connect experiences they've had and synthesize new things. And the reason they were able to do that was that they've had more experiences or they have thought more about their experiences than other people."

Steve Jobs believed that creative people weren't smarter than anyone else, the just had more experiences and thought more deeply about those experiences. For Jobs, each experience was a dot that someone could connect something else to, and for him, it was the connecting of things in unexpected ways that was creative.

Of course, there are a lot of ways to get new experiences. Sometimes, you have to use the experience of others. Read a book, watch a movie, go to a restaurant with food you've never tried, go to a local tourist spot that you've never been to, travel, take a class at your local community college, volunteer for an agency that will put you in touch with new people different from the ones you normally associate with... The list of ways to get new experiences in inexhaustive and only limited by your imagination and bank account. Comic conventions can also provide a space for learning new information in exciting ways.

Be Active 1: Go out and do something new. Think about it. Think deeply about it. Then share (#penguinate).

Be Active 2: Don't know where to start looking for a new experience? Check out the following essays and think deeply about what you read. Then do your own research on the subject.

A: Documentary Films

Documentaries done well place the facts of some event, culture or place in front of us. They explore the interactions and connections between various influences like the government, capitalism and perception. The very best documentaries provide insight into the human condition and a way to improve it. Documentaries aren't journalism stories. They come with an agenda, but many of them also provide enough of the truth to become knowledgeable about a subject enough to ask the right questions.

'Done the Impossible': Fans bring 'Firefly' to the big screen

"Done the Impossible: The Fans' Tale of Firefly & Serenity" is an exploration of how "Firefly" went from a cancelled TV show with only 14 episodes to a major motion picture on the strength of its fans. "Firefly" originally aired on Fox, where science fiction goes to die, and is the creation of Joss Whedon. Classified as a Western Space Opera, "Firefly" starred Nathan Fillion Jewel Staite, Alan Tudyck, Adam Baldwin and others.

"Done the Impossible" is essential viewing for fans of "Firefly" and "Serenity" or anyone who wants to begin to understand what fandom is. Through petitions, letters and other fan actions, as well as the working of Joss Whedon to keep the material and shop it to other companies, the cast and crew were able to get the Serenity off the ground again.

It may be difficult for those outside the phenomenon to understand why people participate in fandoms. Fan groups like The Browncoats allow people to get together and discuss those things that they love best. The Browncoats are also responsible for raising thousands of dollars for Equality Now! a nonprofit that Whedon feels strongly about. They provide a sense of family and a sense of belonging.

The DVD has several awesome special features – the best being the trivia game with Staite, who says good things about the player when the player guesses correctly, and if you are not a fan, it will be a guess. It also has several Easter Eggs. However, what makes it most worthwhile is that Done the Impossible was made by fans; it is their passion that creates a strong documentary.

As Emerald Rose says in Done the Impossible, "Passion is what makes life worth living," and the fans of Firefly and Serenity have enough passion to justify bringing the world of Captain Mal back to life, even if they can't do the same thing with Wash.

Be Active: Watch "Done the Impossible" and find out what it is that drives fans to keep a show alive. Share your thoughts (#penguinate).

'Cave of Forgotten Dreams': Human Art in Prehistory

The "Cave of Forgotten Dreams" explores the oldest cave paintings ever found. At 32,000 years old, the paintings are more than twice as old as any others. After the film shown on April 10, 2012, at the Natural History Museum of Utah and the Utah Film Center, Dr. Laurel Casjens talked about the rock art found in Utah.

"Rock art is something that occurs all over the world," says Casjens. Utah has some very accessible examples of both pictographs and petroglyphs.

Werner Herzog's exploration of the cave is both amazing and kitschy. The best part is that Herzog jumps right into the cave paintings with very little set up. This means that there is very little anticipation left for the rest of the film.

Herzog also explores what life may have been like for the people who did these drawings and lived at the same time as the Neanderthals and mammoths in what is now France.

Unfortunately, Herzog is unable to stay away from his own rambling suggestions of what the cave paintings mean and what they are used for. Instead of allowing the viewer to explore the cave alone, Herzog is there as an all too present guide, who insists on narrating and playing music during what should be an introspective time for the viewer.

The cave will probably not be opened to tourists in our lifetimes, but at least we can explore it through this film, even if we get to deal with our guide.

Be Active: Visit some ancient art near you. Take photos if allowed but don't disturb it. Share (#penguinate).

'Sing Your Song': Harry Belafonte's Life and Times

A biography of musician, actor and activist Harry Belafonte, "Sing Your Song" focuses on Belafonte's roles in numerous activist activities and the results they had in his life. Because of his activist activities during the era of McCarthyism, the FBI broke into his home and told his wife, Marguerite Byrd, that Belafonte was a Communist. Belafonte says in the film that his wife couldn't believe that the government would make up a lie about that, and their marriage dissolved.

He met his second wife, Julie Robinson, when Marlon Brando asked Belafonte to take Brando's girlfriend to lunch. They had many of the same beliefs and interests but grew apart.

As the movie flashes through Belafonte's role in the civil rights movement, in the fight against war and nuclear weapons, in Apartheid and hunger in Ethiopia, in Haiti and its democracy and in gang reform, there is a sense of a repeated pattern. Banners carried in a pre-1973 rally have slogans that could still be used today. Belafonte asks what happened. After 50 years of struggle, why weren't things better?

While he doesn't answer the question, it seems as if the movie would. The great strides that were made in all of those activism activities, of which Belafonte was a part, had to do with his relationship to people. Calling on Hollywood stars to walk with him, to sing, to provide the protection that comes with fame to those who were less famous – he was able to do this because of the friendships he had.

It seems as though relationships matter, especially when he says what he thought about doing before meeting his third wife, Pamela Frank, whom he describes as being someone he is able to spend the rest of his days with.

Be Active: What's your song? Sing it and share (#penguinate).

Films that are based on actual events can stretch the truth pretty far for the sake of the story. "Lone Survivor" features an argument over the ethics of letting the prisoner go that helped explain the Geneva Conventions to the movie audience, but according to the subject of the film, the argument never happened. The Marines involved knew what they had to do and did it. That doesn't mean that these films don't have value; it just means we need to look at them more deeply and examine what's true and what's embellished for effect.

'Lone Survivor': When Hollywood Gets in the Way of Truth

In "Lone Survivor," there is an intense argument about what to do with the Afghanis on the hill. The four Marines run into some goatherds. They take them hostage, tie them up and then have to decide whether or not to kill them.

Ethically, and by the Geneva Conventions, soldiers are not supposed to kill noncombatants. Yet, to release the three goatherds would result in the goatherds telling the Taliban where the Marines were. To not release them would mean their death due to exposure or wild animals. That is where the argument occurs.

However, according to the only person who survived the ordeal, that argument never happened. All four men were immediately on board with the idea that they had to let these goatherds go in spite of knowing the very real and dire consequences.

The director's excuse was that the audience had to understand what was at stake in order for the movie to have any impact. Rather than having an argument about whether or not to kill the goatherds, the script could have been written to have the men discuss the consequences of letting the goatherds go and what they needed to do to survive.

It might have been a little less intense for that discussion, but it would have enhanced the feelings of pride to know that the soldiers in the U.S. Marine Corps were ready to do what is right in that instance regardless of personal consequences.

The truth should be more powerful than the lie, and in this case, it would have been. Better yet, it would have enhanced the reputation of every Marine involved in the incident.

Be Active: Watch "Lone Survivor." Share your ideas from the film (#penguinate).

'Shattered Glass' and Ethics

"Shattered Glass," the film about Stephen Glass and his unethical behavior, should give every journalist pause for thought. Not only about the easy ethics but also the things that may be a little more difficult.

Ethics cannot be regulated through rules. If someone hasn't thought about the ethics of a situation before he or she is in it, he or she may make the wrong ethical decision depending on the pressure that is intrinsic in the situation.

As portrayed by Hayden Christensen, Stephen Glass didn't have any problem with ethics because he was at his core unethical. It is clear from the beginning of the film that something is not quite right with Glass. Because the story is told from his point of view, it is hard to figure out exactly what it is, and most of the things that he does would be thoughtful coming from someone else. Coming from him, it seems a little creepy and possibly manipulative.

It is Glass' manipulative behavior that informs his ethics. He loves being loved by his coworkers, and the best way for him to do get their love and admiration, aside from the almost inappropriate comments and the stalker like memory of how cold his coworker likes her Coke and why she doesn't use ice, is to pitch a good story followed up by false modesty about it. The keyword is "good," which doesn't necessarily mean "truthful."

Glass remains unrepentant for his lying and his manipulation through to the end of the film. This should bother most journalists. An honest mistake, a false fact or a misleading source may happen in the career of a journalist, but the journalist should not be the cause of misleading the public. Those who report the news have an obligation to report the truth regardless of how dull it may be.

Be Active: Journalists aren't the only ones with an obligation to tell the truth and act ethically. What's your guide for ethical behavior and how do continue to follow it in the face of opposition and the easy path? Share (#penguinate).

"The Monuments Men": What Is Art Worth?

Based on a true story, "The Monuments Men" takes on the subject of war from a very different perspective than "Lone Survivor." During World War II, eight men are tasked with saving art from the destruction that the war has caused. The object is to find stolen art and return it to its owners – there is also something about protecting architecture, but that gets thrown out with the first statement of a commanding officer on the ground.

The question that the film asks, and answers in part, is "Why is it worth a man's life to save this art?"

"The Monuments Men" hits all of the right emotional notes. It is possible that the contrast of the beauty of art serves to heighten the sense of horror in war though those horrors are treated only secondarily as the film focuses on the men who were not necessarily on the frontline.

This is a cute little film that misses all of the pageantry, glory and gore of a "Schindler's List" or a "Saving Private Ryan" or even an "Inglourious Basterds." That is where its strengths are. The quiet allows the unsaid to shout deafeningly at the audience. It is the innuendo and suggestion that makes this film a good commentary on the war, life and what they mean.

You may find yourself asking, "What kind of film is this? A war film? A buddy film? An ensemble?" It doesn't matter because it is a good film, and it tells one of those stories that is more important to the survival of who we are than we could ever know. If these men would not have been there saving art, we may still live, but our lives would be less for the loss.

We can only hope that we never have to call on this type of man ever again, but if we do, then we can only hope that our leaders will have the foresight to call on them, that they will exist and that they will heed the call.

The Monuments Men stars George Clooney, John Goodman, Matt Damon, Cate Blanchett, and Bill Murray.

Be Active: What is Art Worth? Share your insights (#penguinate).

Documentary films aren't the only way to learn about life, the universe and everything. Mainstream movies are filled with opportunities to learn something, even if they are bad. You just have to know what you're looking for. Is it how the story is told? What camera angles are chosen and why? Or how did this get on the screen? Maybe, you want to know what the story is trying to communicate. Whatever it is, when you watch a movie, or TV show, think deeply about it.

'Man of Steel': Cold, Hard, Good

Ugh! Another reboot of another superhero franchise. Honestly, how many different ways are there to tell the story of Superman's origins? Wasn't "Smallville" enough? While those may have been my thoughts and the reason why I didn't see "Man of Steel" in the theaters in spite of the fact that Amy Adams is in it, Zack Snyder's take on Superman was really a nicely done movie.

There are still a lot of the same stories as the Christopher Reeve's version of Superman, both the first and second in his series, but overall, in spite of the drag in some places, "Man of Steel" is worth seeing. There are plenty of social issues and moral dilemmas at stake – the energy crisis, what people think about the unknown, how does one become a man, to name a few.

There are plenty of cheesy jokes like the placement of Christ behind Clark's head or the injury report as Zod and Superman battle it out. There is plenty of product placement – most notably Sears, which even my 11-year-old niece picked up on. There were some incongruities, which can be forgive in the context that if the sun granted true invulnerability to the Kryptonians, the movie would have been a lot longer and a lot more expensive to make.

> Spoiler Alert: If you want to know what makes Man of Steel worth watching, keep reading, but know that this is a major spoiler that you have probably already heard about.

However, these drawbacks are to be expected in a big property like "Man of Steel," and as such, they are forgivable if only a little jarring. What truly makes this movie worth watching is the incongruity of watching Superman kill General Zod. Superman is supposed to be the goody two shoes. He has the power and ability to not kill, so he doesn't. It helps keep the villains alive for the next confrontation, and it makes for a good all-around hero.

Henry Cavill's performance, and Adams follow up, are both noteworthy and beautifully done. Unfortunately, the movie glosses over the obvious psychological effects this could have on Clark Kent and goes for the joke at the end rather than explore the nuances. The good news is that this could set up the dynamic that Justice League needs. Superman not wanting to kill people, and Batman being indifferent to the killing. "Man of Steel" is definitely worth a viewing if for no other reason than to prepare for the sequel.

Be Active: You've read my first thoughts on "Man of Steel." Watch it again and form your own opinion and thoughts. Share them (#penguinate).

Refining the 'Man of Steel': What the Frack? Superman Goes Green

In what is clearly the green bias of Hollywood, "Man of Steel" had a not so thinly veiled reference to the energy problems of planet Earth and what is going on in government. Krypton is literally being torn apart because its ruling class decided to harvest the planet's core for energy.

Krypton's leading scientist Jor-El, a man genetically engineered and socially raised to be a scientist, warned the leaders of Krypton of the danger. Yet, even as the planet is exploding in seismic upheaval and the army run by General Zod is staging a coup because of the crisis, the leaders continue to ignore the consequences of their actions. They tell Jor-El that he knows they were out of energy reserves and they didn't have anything else they could do.

This problem is something that had been occurring over the course of decades, and as it got worse, Krypton pulled away from exploring other planets, abandoned already established outposts and left all Kryptonians to be destroyed. They had no backup plan to solve the problem. They just continued to exploit the planet's resources. When Zod breaks into the ruling council's chamber, Jor-El tells him that his way is wrong. Zod claims that they can no longer wait for the ruling council to do their job and that it is a place of endless debates.

If none of this sounds familiar, think about Planet Earth. People continue to exploit natural resources like tar sands and oil shale. Not only do these resources when extracted leave a gaping scar on the land, the process known as "fracking" (which incidentally is a swear word on Battlestar Galactica) has been linked to causing earthquakes and water from faucets that can be lit on fire.

Meanwhile, the army is not necessarily staging a coup, but depots like the one in Tooele, UT, are investing heavily in solar and wind power to save money. Up on Capitol Hill, there are endless debates about something that 97 percent of all scientists now believe to be happening – global warming is a problem, and man has caused it.

"Man of Steel" was one of the highest grossing films of 2013 even with its green message. Maybe it is time to look at the enemies that humans should be fighting. Man versus nature has never been deadlier, but it could be the uniting factor that mankind needs to become a global family.

Be Active: Think deeply about the subject. Avoid sources that provide you with confirmation bias and try to understand the other side of it. What do deniers get out of throwing doubt on climate change and its causes? What do greenies get for expounding their views about the climate and the need for change? Share it if you want, just be aware, you may make people angry no matter which side you come out on (#penguinate).

Refining the 'Man of Steel': What Type of Person Will You Choose to Be?

At a Salt Lake Comic Con Fan X panel, Lisa Mangum talked about the moment where she was hooked on "Doctor Who." In the regeneration episode when David Tennant becomes the Doctor, the Doctor doesn't know what kind of man he is. He fights a bad guy who cuts off the Doctor's hand, and he still gives the bad guy a second chance. In that moment, he says that is the kind of man he is. He has chosen who he wants to be.

> Spoiler Alert: Don't read any further if you plan on seeing Man of Steel.

In "Man of Steel," Clark Kent is faced with the same decision. He is given a framework from his father, Jonathan Kent, especially poignant after Clark saves a bus load of kids and one of the parents shows up at the Kent house frightened.

Jonathan tells Clark that is the reason why Clark needs to keep Clark's powers secret. Clark asks if he should have let the kids die, and Jonathan responds with "Maybe." This is not a strong statement that leads to becoming the selfless Superman of ages gone by. It is the statement of a more cynical era. The right choice for Clark may have been to let a bus filled with children die rather than face the consequences of angry people who do not understand him or his power. Clark is certainly an illegal alien in every sense of the word and one that has powers beyond a normal person.

Later, Jonathan sacrifices himself needlessly to save the family dog and then hide Clark's secret. Clark could have certainly saved Jonathan, but Jonathan expressed his wishes that Clark continue to hide rather than reveal his gifts. In the light of these two incidents, Clark was still told that he decides what kind of man he wants to be. He can choose to aspire to something greater. He just needs to keep testing his limits.

Be Active 1: Watch a movie and come up with two or more thoughts the movie makes you want to explore. Write them down, explore them, and share. Think deeply about the movie and its relation to your thoughts.

Be Active 2: Choose what kind of creator you'll be. Will you be one who hides his or her creative talent, or will you be one that gives his or her creativity for the good of people to the world?

D: Foreign Films

Culture is hard to breakdown and understand. Add to it a language component, and understanding each other in any way is a miracle of sorts. However, as different as cultures and languages are, the human condition is the same. People want to work, have a purpose and enjoy the company of others. People need food, shelter, clothing and love.

Don't let the subtitles throw you off. Enjoy a foreign film and learn about another culture. With the Internet, you don't even have to leave the comfort of your own home. Netflix has hundreds of films and shows from other countries. Many of them are as good as those made in the U.S. Some are even more creative to American eyes.

Be Active: Enjoy a foreign film. Share your recommendation (#penguinate).

A: 'Naparnik': Russia's Buddy Cop Baby Film

If "Freaky Friday" and "Look Who's Talking" had a buddy cop baby film, "Naparnik" ("Partner") would be it. When an undercover detective switches bodies with inept traffic cop's newborn son, it takes almost a year until the undercover detective is able to reveal the truth. The baby with the gravelly voice and his still inept father set out to catch the Dragon and break the curse.

The one-year old looks like he's four, and the CGI treads very close to the uncanny valley where it is difficult to tell whether he is an actual child or a fabrication. However, the uncanniness works because Sergey Garmash's voice coming out of the child's mouth is in and of itself uncanny.

While much of the dialogue was lost on me (there were no subtitles in the theater), the situations were funny: the one-year-old driving a car, and the reaction of the inept cop when a bad guy steps on a flower for specifics. The action was good, too, and the entire movie had me wondering why this concept hasn't been tried in the U.S. Maybe the pitch would be a little weird, but body switching movies, buddy cop films and "Look Who's Talking" all existed at the same time.

If you get a chance to see this, it is worth viewing for a couple of laughs and some scenery from Far East Russia. It is a film full of surprises.

Be Active: Find a Russian film. Watch it. What's different from what you expected? Share (#penguinate).

B: 'White Lion': South Africa's Legend

"White Lion" tells the legend of Letsatsi a rare white lion that the Shangaan believe will bring peace and prosperity to all the creatures of the land. Gisani, a tribesman who grew up listening to the tales of the white lion finds Letsatsi as a cub in trouble and watches over him for the night until Letsatsi is reunited with its mother.

Letsatsi encounters several dangers when the "Evil Twins" take over his tribe and chase all of the males out of territory. Not knowing how to hunt, Letsatsi befriends an older male lion, and they work on surviving together.

"Sometimes friends can lead you down dangerous pathways and teach you bad habits," says the narrator as the two investigate a chicken coop.

The film features several scenes of the white lion club chirping and all of the African wildlife that are common to such stories – giraffes, elephants and zebras. The enemies include hyenas, wildfire and man.

There are several scenes that may remind movie-goers of "The Lion King," but this film is less sanitized including flies and meals in all of their glory and a just a touch less of the savagery that may normally be involved. The actual kill is never shown, but the lions will eat. According to the titles at the end of the film, the lion population has gone from 300,000 to 23,000 in 15 years.

Be Active: Explore the legends of another culture. Share an interesting legend (#penguinate).

C: 'El Bulli' Feeding Creativity with Food

El Bulli is a restaurant that is only open for six months out of the year. The other six months, Chef Ferran Adria and his team spend experimenting with new ideas for food to serve at the molecular gastronomy venue.

"You can eat there three years in a row and not taste the same thing twice," says Executive Chef Mark Smith of Sysco.

The film opens with Adria licking a sucker in the dark. The sucker and his mouth glow with every lick. It then proceeds from the closing of one year through the experimentation for the menu of the next year and ends with the completion of the next year's service.

The film is fascinating even for those who aren't chefs. It is like watching an old Frankenstein flick and wondering when the Jacob's ladder and the beakers will appear. It is as much about the creative process that can be applied in anyone's work as it is about the food, which is spectacular.

This is a high concept film that relies more on images than on words to convey the meaning. There is no narrator to tell the audience what they are seeing or what they should be thinking, and that is the way it should be.

Anyone who likes food or likes the idea of food as a main character in a science fiction film should check out "El Bulli: Cooking in Progress."

Be Active: Cook something you've never made before. Share the results (#penguinate).

Books have the power to take us places while allowing our imaginations to do the work. While movies and other media are fine enough options, books provide us with the opportunity to practice one of the basic qualities creativity needs – imagination. Read a book and go places you can't go, meet people you'll never meet and improve your empathy for others. Of course, thinking deeply about what you read is important to the act of reading.

If you're an avid reader of one genre or a couple of genres, it's time to step out of your zone. Pick up something you wouldn't normally read. Bonus points for finding an independently published author to support. There are plenty of them on Patreon, Bookbub, Goodreads and Amazon.

Be Active: If you need more motivation to read, see if your local bookstore and/or library has an adult summer reading program. Win cool prizes, get invited to a cool party and have a reason to read outside your comfort books.

Still not sure where to start? Here are a couple of my recommendations:

‘Sugar Coated’ Dystopia

Shannen Crane Camp’s “Sugar Coated” introduces Brynn, the lone questioner of the status quo in a seemingly perfect society, and draws us through her questioning into a world that is both idyllic and sinister. It is the contrasting values that bring out the darkness in a world of light, the savor in the sweet and the danger of going through life without ever asking the hard questions.

Camp takes time to build the world of Halcyon. The reader experiences life through the eyes of Brynn, and that limits the perception of what can be told. The exposition never comes off as if there is something that must be explained, but rather it is done in a tone that fits Brynn’s character.

And character is one of the strengths of Camp’s work in this book. All of her characters are created in such a way that they are true to their motivations which do not waver. Brynn seeks truth. Jonah seeks adventure, and Ty seeks only to protect Brynn.

Camp describes her world in terms of vivid colors and strong smells. There are times when it seems that the reader can feel the breeze and smell the air.

Once Brynn and the reader discover the truth that Brynn has been seeking, the book is too close to ending. Fortunately, “Sugar Coated” is part of a trilogy. Readers who want to experience a world that is not what it seems should delve into this smartly written dystopian novel.

Be Active: Question the status quo and do something to change it. Share (#penguinate).

Buddhism meets the Zombie Apocalypse in 'Rebirth: A Zombie Tale'

Darren Lamb writes books that are both profound and entertaining. He stuffs so much wisdom in so few pages that it is amazing that he can do so without seeming to condescend to the reader or the characters. "Rebirth: A Zombie Tale" is no different.

Approaching the zombie apocalypse as a Buddhist, Ryan a follower of Buddhism is chosen to go on a quest to find the reincarnation of his teacher somewhere in Seattle. In order to do so, he has to face the horrors of what has happened to mankind while he was meditating in a monastery in Nepal. If facing the zombie hordes and man's inhumanity to man wasn't enough, Ryan also has to face Mara the destroyer, a woman intent on the destruction of his humanity.

The philosophical conversations are easy to relate to and fascinating. The basic question is "What is humanity?" However, Lamb also addresses why people continue in the face of impossible odds and grief, and he relates stories that illustrate his points with an easy writing style and that draws the reader in.

"Rebirth: A Zombie Tale" features adult themes, sex and violence. It is vividly written and may make some people queasy as it describes the horrors of the dead come to life and the fulfilling of their appetites. This zombie tale also features humor amidst the horror, likable characters and an ending that provides more questions than answers, which is just what everyone needs.

Be Active: Where would you be in the zombie apocalypse? Create something about it. Share (#penguinate).

'As I Knew Him: My Dad, Rod Serling' Cultural Survey and Biography

In her powerful and personal biography "As I Knew Him: My Dad, Rod Serling," Anne Serling presents a cultural survey of America with her father as the way to create a thread that combines all of the elements that took place during his lifetime. This is possible because Rod was outspoken, intelligent and experienced life in America in a way that few people have.

From Rod's experiences in World War II that shaped him as a writer and a person, to the deaths of JFK, Martin Luther King Jr. and Bobby Kennedy, to the election of Nixon as president and to the Vietnam War, the facets of American life are explored through the life of the family and thus avoid the sanitation of the classroom.

The telling of these stories is also possible because Anne loves her father enough to tell the story from her point of view. She takes us through recent American History with a master writer and intelligent man as seen through the eyes of his daughter.

While Anne wrote this book in response to the idea that Rod was "the Angry Young Man of the Golden Age of TV," it is easy to understand how he may have gotten that reputation outside of the home. Rod was adamantly opposed to prejudice and censorship of any kind, and he was outspoken about it.

At home, he was a practical joker who loves children and animals and has more than one nickname for Anne. It is the details that Anne is able to recall and the present tense that the story is told in that brings Rod Serling to life. "As I Knew Him" is a powerful introduction to the person behind "The Twilight Zone" facade. The book inspires a greater respect for Rod and creates a greater connection to his writing.

Be Active: Read a story from "the Twilight Zone" and then watch the episode it's based on. What were the differences. Why did you choose this story? Do you have a favorite "Twilight Zone" episode? Share (#penguinate).

F: Continuing Education

You don't have to go to your community college to continue classes; though if you can, you should. There are plenty of other options online and in your neighborhood, and many of them are free. Kahn Academy has a variety of classes that can be done on your schedule. Don't be afraid that it's supposed to be for teenagers. It's a great way to dive into subjects you don't know or have long forgotten. TED Talks are free. YouTube is free. Vimeo is free. Let's face it: The Internet is full of free places to learn. You just need to know where the information is coming from and whether or not it's true. Never accept anything at face value. Always double check the facts, especially if you find yourself agreeing with it. Challenge your confirmation bias.

If you prefer face-to-face learning, your local library will often host events with speakers. Your local bookstores will likely host authors, who will talk about their books and what's in them. They'll also talk about what they learned from writing and their own life experiences. The community college or university near you will also bring in speakers that are often free to hear.

While they aren't free, community theaters will often present plays of literary merit. The theater going experience is much different than going to the movies. Leave the popcorn at home. Joining a group like Rotary, the Lion's Club, and Kiwanis will support your learning process as will nonprofits like the American Red Cross, where you can learn to save a life and respond to disasters.

Be Active: Find a place to learn something new. Share (#penguinate).

World War I Songs Outnumber Those of Other Wars

The Exploring New Ideas program of the Salt Lake City Public Library brought Michael Lasser in to present "'Til We Meet Again: the Songs of World War I" on November 5, 2011. Lasser, co-author of "America's Songs: The Stories Behind the Songs of Broadway, Hollywood, and Tin Pan Alley," used the evolution of songs during the war to discuss the history of how people felt between 1914 and 1919.

"There were more songs associated with World War I than any other war," says Lasser.

Writers of that era wrote what they knew. They used syncopated tunes that were adopted from African-Americans, conversational lyrics that sounded like the language of speech, and they wrote about love.

"You can write a popular song about anything, but if you can't write a popular song about love, you aren't a songwriter," says Lasser.

Songs like "I Didn't Raise My Boy to be a Soldier" were popular in the U.S. at the beginning of the war in Europe before the United States got involved representing the isolationist thoughts of the average citizen.

When the U.S. entered the war, there were two types of popular songs – expressions of the fighting spirit and the songs that portrayed it as a joke. As the war went on, marshal songs and comedic songs ruled the charts. When the soldiers were returning, songs about how they would adjust came to the fore.

"Nothing gives us a better mirror on what ordinary people were thinking and feeling than the songs they chose to sing," says Lasser.

Be Active: Find a World War I song you love. Share (#penguinate).

Learning through Role-Playing Games

As an avid D&D player from middle school through college, my education was enhanced through the game's complex rules, worlds and math systems. Playing D&D sparked an interest in mythology, mathematics, history, art and, most importantly, it sparked an interest in language and words.

Mythology – D&D is built in the fantasy time of the imagination. While anything can and does exist, it has also taken the gods of several mythologies in Deities and Demigods and quantified who they are, what their powers and realms of control were, and their histories. There may be other comparative mythology books out there, but none are as much fun or as relevant as the D&D version. It allows someone who is already invested in the game to pick up just enough information to want to learn more about the mythologies of the Greeks, the Egyptians, the Norse and several other cultures.

Mathematics – Without math, D&D could not exist as a game that includes random chance. The dice go from 4 sides to 100 sides, and the shapes include a dodecahedron, where else would someone learn what that word means. (It's a 12-sided die in the game.) Experience points, hit points, damage dealt, armor class, what it takes to hit something or perform a task... There are so many mathematical functions that players and Dungeon Masters (DMs), who run the game, need to do in order for the game to go the way it was written, there should be no wonder that it is a game for geeks. Those who get involved in the game become really good at estimating outcomes, adding and subtracting quickly, and being comfortable with numbers. Math is easy when it is used for fun.

History – The weapons used in D&D come from different parts of history. D&D inspires questions like "why is there a difference between a long bow and a short bow?" and "what is a trebuchet?" If a group has to lay siege to a castle, someone has to do the research on how best to do that. The DM runs the game, and so will probably already know the best ways, but the players also have to figure it out. Even though the worlds of D&D are imaginary, they have a basis in the real world. Nothing brings a medieval museum to life like a good D&D game. Stories about wars from long ago come to life when a person has already imagined the weapons and, through the imagination, lived the experience in some way.

Art and Architecture – Drawing is the second form of creativity that children learn. When adults grow up, they insist that they cannot draw. Fortunately for people who play D&D, drawing is not something that is scary or has to be done in a certain way to be desirable. The most basic of drawings can get the idea of what a player wants his or her character to be, and that is something everyone can appreciate. Much like Napoleon Dynamite's Liger, the drawing doesn't have to be realistic to be great.

At some point in a character's growth, the player will want to construct a dwelling for the character. That means figuring out what type of dwelling, how it will be protected and what it looks like. Real world castle architecture becomes a blue print for the character's home. Crenellations, draw bridges, murder holes, secret exits, cisterns – these words and ideas become more relevant to someone who has to learn them to have fun. Visiting a European castle ruins becomes so much more enjoyable when the person already knows what these things are and what they would look like.

Language – There is no way to play a game based on imagination without words. The DM must convey the world, the way it looks, the way it feels and tastes, the way it smells, to the players who must then accurately describe their actions. In order for things to come to life in a shared environment, everyone must have a vocabulary that describes what is in the environment, and the words must mean approximately the same thing to everyone else. A character could pick up a sword, but in D&D unless the players know what kind of sword, its attributes remain a mystery. Is it a short sword, a long sword, an epee, a falchion, a bastard sword...? The list is long, and the more detail that everyone can bring to the gaming table, the livelier the game becomes.

Education doesn't just come from the classroom. It isn't just about learning facts. The best education comes from what a person is interested in and the ability to apply that interest to a real-life situation – even if that real-life situation is only in the imagination of the person. When Michael Jordan spent time on imagining the outcome of free throw after free throw, he was actually improving his free throw success rate. When players and DMs spend time on creating worlds and absorbing the facts of those worlds, they are learning important information about the world outside of the game as well and improving their success rate in the classroom and in future situations requiring creativity.

Be Active 1: Join a role-playing group and learn more about subjects you have little experience with.

Be Active 2: If role-playing isn't your thing, join a group that plays board or card games.

Be Active 3: Join an improv group and push your social boundaries.

'Miss Evers' Boys' exposes Tuskegee Syphilis Experiment

"Miss Evers' Boys" combines stellar acting and a compelling storyline to create a worthwhile theater-going experience. The story is based on the Tuskegee Syphilis Experiment that ran from 1932 until 1972. The experiment was conducted to see the effects of untreated syphilis on the negro male and to be able to compare that to a similar study done in Oslo, Norway. The experiment continued even after penicillin was discovered to be an effective treatment against syphilis.

Eunice Evers, a black nurse who is charged with administering health care and tests to men in the study, cares for her "boys," the black men she deals with in the study, and wants to do what is best for them. She is conflicted about the program and grows ever more concerned as the test goes further "over the hill."

Caleb Johnson is angry and mistrustful of the study he is a part of and is a foil worthy to be Miss Evers companion. Willie Johnson frames the second half of the play. As Willie goes from a champion gillier to suffering the effects of syphilis as it takes away his mobility, the play sinks into the dark depths of inhumanity. Hodman Bryan falls into madness, and both Hodman and Willie cry out on stage each during their own personal tortures that syphilis imposes on them.

The testing that was done to these men is unforgivable, and this play shows the dangers of good intentions and going along with the people in charge. While the play is about a time in American history that most may want to forget, it does give the hope that if people know this story, they can stop the next injustice.

The Talkback

On Feb. 11, 2012, the EttaGrace Black Theatre Company held a talkback after the matinee performance of "Miss Evers' Boys." The talkback featured the actors and director of the play as well as Jeff Botkin, associate vice president for research integrity at the University of Utah.

"I had no clue about this story," says Ricardo Eugene, the actor who played Hodman Bryan. "It is a part of our history, and it is something we don't ever want to repeat."

Botkin says that the study "came to light at a time when the nation was involved with civil rights. It found fertile ground for civic outrage."

Until the revelation of this study, there were no guidelines for ethics in scientific studies.

"It's hard to overstate the impact of this one study on research," says Botkin. It brought about the peer review process, informed consent and the yearly review process to make sure research is still on target and doing what it set out to do.

"The script brings the humanity to the event," says Richard Scott, artistic director. The people that make these types of decisions are people.

"What's exciting for me is to hear people walking out of the theater and talking about this incident," says Director Toni Byrd.

Be Active: Go see a performance at a theater, especially if there is a talk about it afterwards. Share what you learned (#penguinate).

Ch 8: Find the Humor

Humor has a lot of the same qualities as creativity. You're going in one direction until the punchline changes your perception. Finding the humor also brings more optimism and positivity to creativity. Bring out your funny side, and even if you don't create anything more than laughter, you've already done something amazing.

"Hey! Did you see what Rex is doing at the watering hole?"

Bronti was on his way to his afternoon swamp and looked at the tree where Pterry was sitting. "Is he trying to eat everyone again? He knows that doesn't end well for anyone. The last time he ended up tripping and falling head over heels into the pond. Everybody laughed... Until he got out of the water."

Pterry laughed. "That was pretty funny. No, he isn't trying to eat everyone. Well, at least, he isn't trying to eat everyone right now, but he is building something that he says will turn the world into his personal food basket. He was pretty serious about it, too. He even concluded with a maniacal laugh."

"Maybe I'll detour in that direction and see what is up."

"Whatever it is he is building is pretty awesome. I'll meet you there." Pterry took to the sky leaving a shower of leaves to fall below him.

Bronti lumbered in the direction of the watering hole. He figured it would be pretty safe. The watering hole was neutral territory for the most part, and Rex had eaten Steg a couple of days ago, so chances were he wasn't that voraciously hungry. If worse came to worst, Bronti could always use his tail to keep Rex at bay, but he didn't expect it to get that far.

At the watering hole, Bronti could see Rex standing in front of a structure that looked like it was made from a bunch of hollow logs with a flower at the top. Inside the logs were a bunch of mammals that most dinosaurs just ignored. Bronti figured Rex probably thought of them as a snack.

"Hey, Rex, what's up?"

Rex looked up from what he was doing. "Hey, Bronti, I finally figured out what these ridiculously small hands are for. I have been able to construct something that will make every other dinosaur jealous, for at least as long as they survive." Rex laughed maniacally.

Bronti looked around for Pterry and saw him in a tree shrugging.

"So, you put a bunch of trees together and that giant flower there and what are you going to do with it?"

Rex tilted his head as far down as he could and stretched out his arm – it was just enough for him to be able to scratch his chin. "You know, I am almost always hungry. This device will turn the world into my food basket. I won't have to even hunt. I will just be able to walk from carcass to carcass and eat my fill. Look, it's almost ready. Let me just get these mammals started, and you can see it in action." Rex gave the mightiest roar that Bronti had ever heard. The mammals were so scared that they scampered in directions that turned the logs against each other.

Lightning sparked. Rex roared again. The mammals ran faster. The lightning got bigger. Rex roared again, and the mammals ran as fast as they possibly could. The machine whirred and ground and squeaked and crunched as wood rubbed against wood. Then a single beam of light as bright as the first rays of the sun shot forth from the flower at the top and into space.

"EUREKA!" Rex did a little dance. "The world will be my food basket! Nice knowing you, Bronti. I'm sure I will be having you for dinner soon."

Bronti snickered at the notion.

"Now, I am going to have a nap and wait." Rex pushed down the contraption and wandered into the forest.

Bronti looked at Pterry. "What was that about?"

"I have no idea." Pterry shrugged. "I think Rex has finally lost it. It did look pretty though."

"Well, I'm going back to the swamp. See you, Pterry."

Pterry waved goodbye and flew away.

Three days later, there was a flash of light in the sky followed by the trembling of an earthquake. The sky grew dark, and the dinosaurs began to die off. Rex's machine had work. Rex ate well for the coming months until he, too, ran out of food and died of hunger. The greed of one dinosaur had destroyed life for all of the other dinosaurs on the planet.

That's dinovation. It didn't go extinct with the dinosaurs, but it might go extinct with us.

Be Active: What's your favorite dinosaur? Why? What adaptations did it have to cope with life among the giants? Share (#penguinate).

B: A Turkey Pan Shall Light the Way

The rain that had fallen earlier in the evening gave the road a glossy blackness that seemed to absorb the light from the headlights on my car. The heavy cloud cover kept the sky darker than it should have been on a late autumnal night.

My friends and I had spent the evening in Portland entertaining ourselves with nickel video games, a movie and a small shopping spree that included items for Thanksgiving dinner.

The weather was misty, but there was no fog – just dark.

Boom! The wheel jerked in my hand, but I kept control of the car.

"What was that?" asked Rob who was sitting in the passenger seat.

"I think I blew a tire," I said as I pulled to the side of the road.

We piled out of the car. Sure enough the rear driver's side tire was flat.

"No problem," I said, "I'll have this changed in no time." I opened the trunk and pulled out the spare and the jack. "Steph, can you get my flashlight out of the glove compartment?"

Stephanie went to the passenger side of the car to get the flashlight.

I got my jack under the car and lifted it up.

"Umm, Shad, where did you say that flashlight was?"

"In the glove compartment."

"It's not there."

I looked at the tire. I couldn't see anything. After confirming that there was no flashlight available, I asked, "Does anyone have anything reflective?" Again, the answer was negative. "Okay, we do this the hard way. It's going to take a little longer than I thought." I popped off the hubcap and tried to find the first lug nut. A car passed by and gave me just enough light to get crossbar positioned to remove the lug nut. "I just need a little more light." I struggled with the next lug nut until I noticed that I could see – just a little better. My eyes must have adjusted.

The rest of the operation was simple. I could see just enough to change the tire without any real problems. When I was done, I looked at those around me. "Where's Stephanie?"

"I am over here." She was standing at the headlights holding the turkey pan we had purchased earlier in the day so that it reflected just enough light for me to change the tire.

Be Active: What was the best way you or a friend have ever solved a problem? Share (#penguinate).

"Unhand that cow!" The knight in full armor sat atop his huge warhorse, sword drawn and pointed at the peasant leading a cow down the road. His squire stood next to the horse holding a banner, red with a charging bull on it.

The peasant was terrified – so terrified, in fact, that he couldn't release the reins of the cow.

"I will only ask one more time, knave." The warhorse reared up. "Unhand that cow, now." He flourished his sword menacingly.

The peasant dropped to his knees and began stammering – the reins still in his hand.

"Well, if that is the way it is to be…"

The squire interrupted his liege, "Sir, perhaps you will let me talk to this peasant?" The knight nodded his assent; the squire walked toward the peasant. "You were planning on taking this cow to the slaughterhouse?"

The peasant nodded his head.

"We cannot allow that." The squire took the reins from the peasant and handed him a few coins. "The knight there is sworn to eat no beef and to protect cattle wherever he may find them." The squire returned to the knight. The peasant walked away with more money than he had ever seen.

"Well done, squire. Now we must hurry to the tournament."

"Yes. My lord, your nephew waits."

The squire and his knight arrived at the tent where the nephew was waiting. The knight descended from his horse as his nephew rose to greet him. They exchanged pleasantries and talked about some of the adventures they had had since they last met.

A rather fat man entered the tent and addressed the squire, "Gird up your Loins; the Elder is due in the lists and the Younger is due in the circle of swords."

The squire bowed as the fat man left. Scooping up the two banners – one with a charging bull, the other with a pawing bull – and grabbing their weapons, the squire announced, "Sir Loin the Elder, here is your lance; Sir Loin the Younger, here is your sword. Your presences are requested on the field."

Be Active: Creativity doesn't always bring the type of renown we'd like. If you're creativity has brought you notoriety, even if it wasn't in the way expected, accept it and keep creating. Share your experience (#penguinate).

Ch 9: Be Childlike

Creativity often comes from people who haven't lost their childlike qualities: curiosity, playfulness, and a willing to experiment. The joy in examining the details at the borders of the playground or jumping in a puddle just to see what water would do are a part of childhood. As people get older, it becomes uncool to indulge in childlike activities. Adults shouldn't jump in puddles; it'll ruin socks and shoes. Being childlike is looked down upon as being childish. However, the two are entirely different.

Comic conventions are one great way to indulge the inner child. Dress in costume and revel in childhood memories while meeting your childhood heroes. Disney parks invite adults and children alike to play. However, having a tea party at home can bring out much of the child in you. Visiting a local nickel arcade can invite you back to childhood arcade games and air hockey. Playing with your dog or cat while not feeling obligated to do so can also harken back to younger days.

Be Active: Get together with your inner child and make a pact to get in touch with his or her good qualities. Explore like a child. Be curious and play like a child. Swing on the swings, look at the bugs, and take a splash in a puddle. Share (#penguinate).

A: Get Dressed Up

On 4 Dec. 2016 at Malta Comic Con, Chiara Cardello and Giulia Sulsenti talked about cosplay budgets and competitions. Much of the discussion was translated through Fabio Agius.

More money doesn't necessarily mean a better costume. Low budget costumes made from cardboard covered in foam and PVA glue or papier mache can be as good as those costumes made from more expensive materials.

"Finishing is the most important thing" in a costume, says Cardello.

Foam should be sanded to make it smooth and then covered in PVA glue to fill in the imperfections of the foam. It should then be sanded again. Never apply acrylics directly to the foam. Many Maltese costumes weren't sanded enough.

Cardboard can be prepared quickly, but it is important to pay attention to details. If the details aren't done right, the costume will look like it was put together in a hurry. Looking at things that can be recycled and used in the costume will help keep costs down. Two layers of an inexpensive textile can make it look more expensive.

Cosplay competitions are equally about the costume and the act. Cosplayers should feel their characters and become them.

Be Active: Make a costume and share it (#penguinate). Bonus for wearing it to a comic convention near you and participating in the cosplay contest.

B: Seeing Childhood Heroes: Buck Rogers and Twiki

Gil Gerard and Felix Silla paired up to do a panel on "Buck Rogers in the 25th Century" at Emerald Valley Comic Fest on Oct. 3, 2015. Gerard said that the best thing about doing the show was the paycheck every week. When the show changed executive producers between the first and second seasons, Gerard knew that something familiar was going on with the plot.

"I was such a sci-fi numbskull," says Gerard. "I thought they ripped off Star Trek." The show was ripping off Battlestar Galactica, which had just been canceled.

Gerard had his own idea for the show and pitched it to Brandon Tartikoff. Had the show gone a third season, it is likely that Buck Rogers would have been on a journey to find out who he was in his new time period.

When he was starting out, Gerard moved to New York to become an actor after finding himself bored as an industrial chemist in charge of other people.

"You don't move to New York just to be a cab driver," says Gerard. He drove for about six months before he could make a living with acting. "I wore out two soles of shoes looking for work."

Gerard chose New York because in Los Angeles, actors need an agent to get work, work to get film and film to get an agent.

"In New York, you didn't need an agent to work," says Gerard. He worked on Broadway in shows like "Carrousel" and "Oklahoma" where he played Curly.

Gerard says that the business cycle for actors runs like this:

- Who's Gil Gerard?
- Get me Gil Gerard.
- Get me the Gil Gerard type.
- Who's Gil Gerard?

It is one thing to get to the top and another thing to stay there, and Gerard is proud of the respect that his peers give him.

The iconic roles that Gerard turned down included the lead in "Moonlighting" because he didn't want to work opposite of Cybil Shepherd at the time, "Scarecrow and Mrs. King" and "Magnum P.I." In his free time, Gerard writes, and he golfs with his wife and a remote-control cart he named Twiki.

Felix Silla

Gil Gerard says that Buck Rogers was lucky to cast Felix Silla in the role of Twiki. The suit was made out of fiberglass and hard rubber.

"He created a character, that people had an opinion on, through two inches of plastic," says Gerard.

Silla went through an interview process and thought the best thing was that filming took place five minutes from his home.

"We had a lot of fun," says Silla.

Silla also played the role of Cousin It on "The Addams Family." He went in for the interview on a Friday, and they told him to come back on Monday for the job.

"They pick whoever they want," says Silla of the casting process. Silla later played in the Original Harmonica Band.

Be Active: Try out for a production. Find your local community theater or a nearby casting call, even if it's just as an extra on a TV show. Share (#penguinate).

C: Get Animated

Alba Garcia-Rivas' "Time Space Reflections" is art. Dedicated to twin sisters, one of whom died tragically young, "Time Space Reflections" uses stop motion animation to tell the story of twin sisters who find each other through space and time. One uses technology to build a portal while the other uses magic. When they see each other, they recognize that they are related and they were searching for one another. They want to meet face to face, but going through the portal could be deadly.

The story is told without dialogue as the puppets, which were changed after each shot, emote their desires through well-choreographed movements and facial expressions. The 8-minute run time does not do the film justice. It is beautifully done and deserves more, especially since I feel like I am a better person for having seen the film.

"Time Space Reflections" was made in Garcia-Rivas' basement in the Bronx. Her team of people at the top of their professions included special effects personnel and stop motion pioneers. Many of them volunteered to work on the film because of Garcia-Rivas' passion and persistence. 11,000 photos were made for the 8-minute film. Garcia-Rivas and her team are working on "Dangerously Ever After" for the next film. She says that her current needs include a warehouse so that she can store all of the sets and props.

Be Active 1: If you shy away from animated films, it's time to change your tune. Even if you don't like Disney films, you can choose from Blue Sky, DreamWorks, or any of the anime films available to American audiences. Choose a film and look for the artistry, story and music in the film. Share your experience (#penguinate).

Be Active 2: Make your own stop motion, or otherwise, animated film and share it (#penguinate).

Ch 10: Replenish the Well

Everyone needs to take a break sometime. Some Americans take pride in never having a day off of work. For creatives, however, that type of thinking can lead to burnout, illness and creative blocks. Not only do you need a day off from your creative endeavors, you have to find a way to replenish your creative well. For some, it's easy to replenish the well. Ray Bradbury created an office space cluttered with ideas where he would never starve for lack of idea creation. Some creators are able to take a day off, and mean taking off the time between sunrise and sunset and writing in the evening as a change from their normal routine.

Even if you're brimming with ideas and have notebooks filled with them, rejuvenating your creativity will make those ideas easier to implement and explain. It will even make them better. So, what do you do to improve your creativity while refilling your creative well? Travel is one of the most often mentioned ideas for creatives.

Travel takes you away from the day-to-day interruptions that come with being a creative and puts you in the way of new cultures, new experiences and a place to relax and enjoy yourself. While travel by itself won't make you more creative. Thinking deeply about your experiences on vacation will. Even if you can't travel out of the country, you can take a drive into the country. Find a city or town that you've never been to and enjoy its history, tourist attractions and parks.

If that seems too far off. Read about a new place, watch a travel show and eat food you've never tried before. Combine the food with the travel show about a place where the food originated, and you'll get a richer experience.

Be Active: Go somewhere new, about 60 miles away, and share something about it (#penguinate).

A: Disneyland

Everyone has his or her own happy place – a place where the person can recharge and feel more like the person that he or she is rather than the one that the world perceives. For me, it's the magic of Disneyland that helps me recharge. Memories of childhood and new magical discoveries are just a quick trip away, and even two days is enough for me to drop the weight of the world and the stress of bills. I understand that not everyone loves Disneyland, but if you've never been there and you need a place to replenish your well, go, be childlike and enjoy the magic.

World of Color – Winter Dreams 2013

"The World of Color – Winter Dreams" delivers Disney magic in a big way. Hosted by Olaf the Snowman, the show is a masterpiece of cinematic presentation and technical know-how. Compiled from winter scenes of Disney animations including ice skating by Mickey and Minnie and Bambi's first experience with a frozen lake. Winter Dreams also has original animation.

Its best moments come from a 2-dimensional Olaf, and a Toy Story reinterpretation of the Nutcracker, wherein the aliens who worshipped the claw dance just like the mushrooms in Fantasia until Rex gets involved, and where Jessie dances with Woody in a repetitive and still extremely comical way. More serious moments are highlighted by the show-stopper "Let It Go" by Elsa from "Frozen."

These moments alone would have been worth going to the show for. However, the absolute pinnacle of the show is the creation of snowflakes that are at least a foot in diameter. Watching the snowflakes come out of Christmas presents gives me the same feeling that people who saw Abraham Lincoln come to life in 1964 must've felt. This is what Disney does second best. It gets technology to become something more. (First best is that it gets people to be happier – employees and guests alike.)

Be Active: Make your own snowflake. Share (#penguinate).

The Submarine Voyage (1959 to 1998)

One of the first experiences of Disney magic that I remember was that of the original Submarine Voyage, or at least the one that existed from the late '70s to the late '90s.

I knew by watching the subs from above that they never really descended any farther into the water. They did disappear into a cavern, but being on the ride and knowing when the subs descended, my young mind knew that it corresponded to a certain section of the lagoon.

Yet, when I was actually on the ride, I was entirely convinced that the subs were actually sinking. My own senses told me that we were going underwater, and I could find nothing beyond the logic that was being trumped by actual experience to help me understand what was going on.

As I grew older and somewhat taller, I finally figured out how the illusion was created. Breaking the illusion didn't make the old ride any less attractive. I enjoyed experiencing it because of the memory of the riddle that those subs brought to me, and the joy that went with not being able to solve that riddle.

Plus, I really like corny jokes, the mermaids and that goofy looking sea serpent. I am sad that the ride was converted to a Finding Nemo theme, but I can always remember the magic that I experienced when I was young, and that is part of the magic of Disney.

Be Active: Share your favorite corny joke (#penguinate).

Mickey Mouse Foods and Happiness

At Disneyland, you can Mickey Mouse everything. From the ice cream bars that Grahms loves to cupcakes with Mickey Mouse confetti, everything can be made in the shape of Mickey Mouse. Perhaps the best of these treats come for breakfast. At the River Belle Terrace, you can get a Mickey Mouse pancake, and at the Carnation Café (Oscar's), you can get a Mickey Mouse waffle. Make no mistake, these gimmicky treats are not just for children. They are for the young at heart, and with the right person, they are downright magical.

During the solo part of my trip in 2013, I went to Oscar's for breakfast like I normally do. A couple in their mid-20s sat at the table beside mine. When her Mickey Mouse waffle arrived, she squealed with delight and was so excited about the presentation that she could not contain herself. It was her genuine joy that made her, in that moment, the perfect woman.

That kind of joy is hard to find in real life where the world seeks out what is wrong rather than trying to find the joy in the simple things. You will find what you seek. Fortunately, Mickey Mouse pancakes can be made in your home. You might have to buy some fruit, but other than that, all it takes is pancake batter.

Be Active 1: Share the magic of your favorite Disney or other theme park experience (#penguinate).

Be Active 2: Share an effect, whose inner workings you understand and you still find amazing (#penguinate).

Be Active 3: Make pancakes in your favorite shape as long as it's not circular! Share (#penguinate).

B: Malta

The island nation of Malta played a pivotal role in World War II and the defeat of the Nazis, but its history extends to far earlier times. From Phoenician traders to the Roman Empire, Malta mixes influences from other cultures including the French and the English. St. Paul wrecked on the island, and Gozo, one of the islands in the archipelago, allegedly was the home of Circe, who trapped Odysseus there. The Turks attacked the Knights of St. John and were defeated in 1565 by those Maltese Knights. Prehistoric temples abound, including the oldest free-standing structure in the world, and a treasure trove of bones at Ghar Dalam from animals that adapted to their home as the island was cut off from Europe's mainland.

For a country that is made of 3 inhabited islands, one of which boasts 4 permanent residents and the largest of which is 15 miles across, Malta is an amazing country that offers plenty to think about. The people are nice. The food is good, and the University of Malta offers degrees in Creativity and Innovation at its Edward de Bono Institute, named for a leader in creativity and innovation research and thinking. A thriving film industry has left its mark with Popeye Village, and Playmobil has its factory located in the country where it manufactures its Playmobil figures.

If you want history and adventure in an English-speaking country, Malta is the place to go. Its warm weather and amazing lightning storms are an added bonus, as is Malta Archery with leading Instinctive Archery Master Armin Hirmer and the amazing Malta Comic Con, now more than 10 years old!

The Hypogeum 2014

In the dark underground of the Hypogeum huddled together with 10 other people, you can almost imagine what the people who came before thought about while they were busy carving the walls and rooms of this ancient site. Whatever you imagine could be what happened here because there haven't been enough pieces put together to say what the area truly was.

What We Know for Sure

When the Hypogeum was finally excavated, after having houses built over the top of it, the remains of 7,000 bodies were found. They were all jumbled up leading to the idea that the place was a tomb of sorts.

Archaeologists also found several different figurines, including Malta's own "Sleeping Lady." Many of the figurines are gender ambiguous. No one can say if they were placed there in reverence or if they were thrown in with the bodies.

The Hypogeum is the first example of sculpture as architecture. Early man carved away at the stone to create the illusion of architecture. Technically, this makes the Hypogeum a sculpture or a series of sculptures. So much care was used in the carving to take advantage of the rock's natural strength, that the structure has survived several earthquakes throughout its 6,000-year history.

The carved rocks resemble several of the above ground temples on Malta. As the only example of an intact roof, the Hypogeum provides an insight to what those roofs looked like.

It is super fun to say "Hypogeum."

Everything Else Is Conjecture

Is this a mass grave, a burial chamber, a site of worship or something else? While some theories are based on what is known about other prehistorical sites, it is important to remember that there is a reason that it is called prehistory. No one can say anything about what the site was used for with 100 percent accuracy. At the Hypogeum, this lack of information is exacerbated by the disturbance of the site long before it was reported as being discovered.

The Experience

In order to protect the delicate micro climate, only 10 people are allowed in the chambers per tour, and there are only about eight tours a day. The tours are nominally led by a docent with every participant receiving what looks like a cell phone to listen to the recorded narration and music. The music was created by a musician who spent considerable time in the chambers.

Be sure to get to know your fellow tour goers as quarters are tight. There are some places that it is important to allow everyone into the area to see what is being illuminated before the lights go out. Also, do not let the maps fool you, the visit is conducted in a very tiny area even if it consists of three levels. And mind thy head, this is one tour where it pays to be short.

No photos are allowed in the Hypogeum, and visitors are asked to leave everything that they might be holding in their hands in a cabinet at the beginning of the tour. Tickets are available online and should be booked in advance. Though some tours are left open, so visitors can get tickets the day before.

The Hypogeum underwent restoration to its micro-climate controller in 2016. Other parts of the tour may have changed as well. Still, this experience is one that you shouldn't miss. Just book ahead.

Be Active: If you can't get to Malta, learn something about its involvement in World War II or about its other historic eras. Share (#penguinate #malta).

Malta Playing Arts

In a brilliant concept, Margit Waas has curated an exhibition of contemporary Maltese art while creating a scathing social commentary on the state of Maltese economics and art at the same time. In the introduction to a deck of cards, Waas explains that the concept came from the need for a contemporary arts museum in Malta. While there are three casinos and over 250 online gaming entities, there is not one contemporary arts museum. This deck represents a permanent and mobile collection of contemporary art from Malta. The Walkthrough and Compendium provided with the deck gives the story behind each of the art works and provides a short but compelling read.

Malta does have smaller contemporary arts galleries like Lily Agius, and it has the National Fine Arts Museum whose modern display of art is severely limited. However, with no specific place to display a variety of contemporary pieces, Malta sends a clear message about what it values and fails to realize that art is one area where the country could excel if it provided its artists not only a place to display their art, but also a way to identify as artists full-time and a way to make a living rather than having to squeeze art in between of everything else that is economically important.

A country of such rich culture and history should realize that art is the way that most of that history has survived and will continue to survive. From the Hypogeum to the portraits of the Grandmasters, art plays an important part in helping future generations understand what went before.

This deck of cards not only cleverly exposes a social problem in Malta, but it also supports Happy Paws, an organization dedicated to helping the strays in the country. Malta has innumerable stray cats that provide protection from rodents and need care. If you want to experience Malta and playing cards through contemporary artists or you want to support kittens and puppies on the islands, this deck of cards is an awesome way to do so.

Be Active: Make your own deck of playing cards. Share (#penguinate).

Be Active 2: Get a deck of Malta Playing Arts. Share (#penguinate #Malta).

Maltese Cuisine

Because of Malta's history, foods have been greatly influenced by the Turks and the Italians. I have yet to try rabbit, but here is my first food survey.

Pastizza (pl. pastizzi) – When made correctly, these little pockets of ricotta are a joy for the palate. Each warm bite of salted ricotta cheese feels like happiness as it fills up your stomach. The filo dough is crispy, flaky and everything that it should be. I don't know what it is about ricotta, but it just tastes like home. When done incorrectly, these turn into an overly doughy, tasteless, flat and wholly unsatisfying food item.

Pastizzi can also be stuffed with peas. I don't know why, but there it is. Peas are healthy, right? The pea filled pastry is good, but given the choice, I choose ricotta unless I know that the ricotta pastizzi are bad. Pastizzi are relatively inexpensive – 30 Euro cents (roughly 50 American cents).

Qassatat (the 'q' is silent) – This pocket of peas has a lot of dough surrounding the peas. I am told that I haven't had a good one of these, yet, but I am not sure why anyone would choose a qassatat over a pastizza.

Kinnie – The Maltese soft drink is labeled as bitter orange with aromatic herbs. If you had the Israeli drink at Epcot's Cool Club, you know what the bitter tastes like after the sweet. Like other drinks, coffee and alcohol, it takes some getting used to. While it is a soda and maybe it would be better if I didn't add it to my calorie count, there is something about the unexpected bash of bitter that keeps me interested in figuring out why I like Kinnie.

Donuts – are available. I am reserving judgment.

Kannoli – TRIUMPH AT LAST! I had a kannoli earlier in the week as the nearest convenience store had some in the case, and I was a bit disappointed. I chalked it up to the fact that no one makes them as good as grandma. The filling was bland, and the crust was moist if not yet soggy.

Then my roommate showed me the Dolceria Josie Bonaci bakery. As I bit into this kannoli, the outer shell snapped, and the insides exploded with beautiful flavors and textures – chocolate chips and candied fruits filled in a void while ricotta created a dreamy separation for the two. This was the kannoli I was searching for. I suspect that I will now be gaining weight though the bakery is just far enough away to make it inconvenient, and I have a budget to maintain. Still... KANNOLI, I mean come on.

Be Active: Make something influenced by Maltese cuisine. Share (#penguinate #Malta).

C: Russia

Russia spans two continents and developed from west to east. Its culture has influences of communism and the tsars. Traveling to Moscow or the Far East is very different not just in language and culture but also in alphabet. It would take more than a couple of years to understand the Russian psyche, but the culture is as rich as the history.

Taking the Train in Far East Russia

Flights out of Blagoveshchensk aren't always convenient when you want to head to the West Coast of the United States. There used to be a flight to Seoul, and there may be one in the future, but when we were looking at flights for heading to Lilac City Comicon 2018, we found that we would have to fly to Moscow first and then back to Khabarovsk. That wasn't going to fly, so we took the train.

The train left in the evening, which meant that the bulk of the travel was done during sleeping hours. This is probably easier for everyone involved because it is so much easier to take care of people who aren't moving about. My wife and I purchased the slight upgrade, and it was worth it. We had our own bunk and only shared the cabin with 2 other people. Baggage can be stowed under the seats.

The cabin itself was modern and posh. The seat cushions were firm, and the train is smoke-free though there was a slight tinge of smoke in the air as if someone had smoked there in the distant past.

The toilet was clean at the outset and stocked with toilet paper and paper towels. The bathroom would not be unfamiliar to the European traveler. At either end of the corridor, there is a sign that notes the time, the temperature outside and whether or not the bathroom is free. Don't read Russian? That's okay because there is a red or green dot that also indicates the occupation, or lack, of the toilet. (Red is occupied; green is empty.) As of our travel dates, all the trains are scheduled and run on Moscow time. This can be confusing to people not living in Moscow's time zone, but it is supposed to change in the near future.

A hot meal is delivered and is generally of higher quality than standard airline food. It won't win any restaurant awards, but it's tasty and filling. We had chicken and noodles with a roll and pastry for dessert.

Two of the beds fold down from the wall, and the other two, fold down over the seats. Each guest gets slippers, towel, toothbrush and toothpaste. A pillow and duvet cover are included and a duvet can be found for each person in the storage area that extends over the corridor. For people who don't mind taking more than a couple of hours to get to their destinations, the train in Far East Russia offers a comfortable and friendly way to travel.

Be Active: Take a train somewhere, anywhere. If you want, find a holiday train or a train at an amusement park. Share your experience (#penguinate).

New Year's Eve in Russia

According to my family, New Year's Eve is the most important holiday in Russia. A combination of the American holidays: Halloween, Christmas and New Year's Eve, the holiday is more family focused than the New Year's Eve parties that many Americans participate in. There is still plenty of drinking as family members toast each other, toast the old year and, when the New Year rolls in, the future. The New Year's Tree is up and decorated. Dyed Moroz (or Grandfather Frost), Russia's version of Santa Claus, stops by before the Old Year is over and brings gifts. Some celebrations feature bags of candy, which are given as gifts, and people in costume. Russians also follow the Chinese zodiac for the year – 2018 is the year of the dog.

Before the bell tolls, the family, and any friends that have stopped by, are in place at the table that is stacked full of food. Our particular celebration included a 12-layer liver stack, herring in a fur coat, potatoes, ribs, carrots with garlic mayonnaise and cheese, Holodets – a meat in jelly dish, and Salties – tomatoes and cucumbers that have been home pickled. Drinks included mors, water, cognac and Russian champagne.

On TV, the Russian channels have variety shows much like Dick Clark's Rockin' New Year's Eve. However, these appear to have been pre-taped because the stars are on all the channels in different outfits. Still, there is singing and humorous sketches. After the bell strikes midnight, Putin gives his New Year's wishes, and everyone congratulates one another on finishing an old year with good wishes for the new one to come. The family may head outside to enjoy personal aerial fireworks.

New Year's Day is considered the day of salads. Leftovers are eaten along with many salads that are mayonnaise or mustard based.

Be Active: Adopt a new tradition at your next celebration. Research how other cultures celebrate and figure out how to add it to your happy day. Share (#penguinate).

Breakfast with the Russians

My wife, who's Russian, gets up ridiculously early to make breakfast. Look, any time someone is up before the sun, it's ridiculously early. During the week, she makes 20-minute oatmeal (because as "My Cousin Vinny" taught us, no self-respecting Russian would use instant oatmeal) with berries and bananas or fried eggs, usually with some sort of herbs and possibly green peppers and tomatoes. On the weekends, she'll make cirniki, pancakes or something else more elaborate. It's all good, but it just takes so much time. I'd be happy with a bagel and cream cheese to go with my coffee if it meant we could sleep in longer, but they don't exist here as far as I can tell.

When I saw the Nesquik tie-in with Disney for Disney's new Russian release "The Last Warrior," I had to get the box of cereal. I sold the idea to my wife as "it'll be an easy way to make breakfast," but she agreed because she knows I like surprises in the form of toys that come with food items. So, when we didn't eat cereal on Monday morning, I was a little disappointed, but my wife likes a warm breakfast, and oatmeal with bananas and berries is actually healthy and tasty.

In the evening, for tea time, I decided I would have a bowl of cereal and my wife and daughter decided to join me. I get out the box, and my wife pours me a glass of milk. I ask why, and she says it's for my cereal. I start to protest, but there's no putting the milk back in the box. I just tell her that we normally pour the milk from the box.

So, the cereal box, the milk, my glass, bowls and spoons go on the table, and my wife starts to pour milk in her bowl.

"WHAT? WAIT! Cereal first, then milk. Otherwise, the cereal just floats on the milk. You'll never get enough that way."

Meanwhile, my daughter grabs the box and pulls the bag all the way out. She is in act of opening it...

"NOOOOOOOOOOO! What are you doing? If you open the bag outside of the box, it will never go back into the box!"

She puts the bag back in the box and rips it right down the center!

"You killed it! Why did you kill it? You're a cereal killer! The bag is supposed to help keep the cereal fresh! AAAAAAAAAAAUUUUUUGGGGH! It's like you've never eaten cereal before!"

My daughter gives me this look that expresses they really haven't and says, "I've seen on shows where they pour the cereal directly from the box."

"Yes, with the bag inside." I saved the bag as best I could. Everyone had cereal and milk and lots of laughter.

Who knew there were so many rules to eating cereal? It's a good thing my family finds me entertaining.

The next morning, the cereal is on the table with the milk. My wife says, "It's so easy. You just put 2 boxes on the table, everyone gets their own spoons and bowls, and it's done. Plus, it makes you happy."

"Yeah, but we can't have cereal every day. It isn't really healthy."

"Honey, happiness is healthy."

Be Active: Travel doesn't always reveal something about the culture where you're at. Sometimes, it reveals more about your own culture. Find an event near you that explores another culture. Explore the foods and entertainment. What do you find surprising? What is different from your everyday? What did you enjoy most? What did you enjoy least? Why? Share (#penguinate).

Be Active 2: Take time to make an elaborate breakfast. Enjoy with someone you care about. Share your experience (#penguinate).

Ch 11: Draw on Life's Experiences

Living life should be more than just going to work and sitting at a desk and then coming home and sitting in front of the television. Experiences provide the basis for all creativity. Even if you feel like all you do is go to work and come home, there can still be inspiration in that experience because creativity and life consist of thinking deeply about those experiences. Scott Adams' "Dilbert" and Manny Trembley's "Unicountant" are two examples of what the average workday has inspired. No matter what your life is like, think deeply about it and create from the experiences.

When the world's biggest toy store declared bankruptcy, it didn't seem like a big deal. Chrysler declared bankruptcy. We still drive their cars. The banks have gone belly up and got bailed out. Some airlines have declared bankruptcy, and still, we fly the friendly skies. So, it seemed like Toys 'R' Us could still have a shot at remaining a part of the retail world. Unfortunately, the toy retailer will be closing all of its stores. Alas, Geoffrey is dead.

Toys 'R' Us was founded in 1969, but its heyday was during the 1980s. When Reagan eliminated children's television regulations, Toys 'R' US and other brands could target children with their advertisements. Marketers found children to be the best motivators for parents to buy anything -- toys, cereal, cigarettes. And Toys 'R' Us loomed large with its Geoffrey the Giraffe mascot standing neck and head above the rest of the riff raff.

Toys 'R' Us was the second happiest place on Earth, and it was a lot closer than Anaheim. Children became Toys 'R' Us kids, and Generation X learned that growing up sucked because you would lose your status and your friend Geoffrey. If you weren't a Toys 'R' Us kid, what were you? A suit-wearing, cubicle-sitting drone engaging in any number of activities that Lloyd Dobler would disparage at the end of the decade. No self-respecting kid would want that.

Whether or not Toys 'R' Us encouraged Gen Xers in their seemingly never-ending childhood, the toy giant played a huge role in U.S. culture. Its jingle remains inside the skulls of children who have seen thousands of hours of cartoons with commercials readily played during breaks. The fear that sat within the hearts of those of us growing up as Reagan rattled the swords could be assuaged and made fun of with the help of Toys 'R' Us. We didn't want to grow up, and we didn't want to blow up; we were Toys 'R' Us kids.

And now that our childhood has collapsed under the weight of its own greed and debt, what are we? Who are all of the Toys 'R' Us kids now? Hopefully, they are people who Lloyd could be proud of. Maybe if we are lucky, we can all still be Toys 'R' Us kids because...

> "From bikes to trains to video games,
> It's the biggest toy store there is. (Gee Whiz!)
> I don't wanna grow up 'cause, baby, if I did,
> I couldn't be a Toys 'R' Us kid.
> More games, more toys, more joys, oh boy!
> I wanna be a Toys 'R' Us kid."

Be Active: If there's something you miss from your childhood, use it to spark your creativity. If there's something you loved that has gone away because of economic issues, use it to create. Share (#penguinate).

Football is war. Two teams battle against each other for every inch, foot and yard of territory. Players crash into each other. The quarterback rifles a shot down the field, and the offensive lineman try to hold the line while the defense attempts to take out the general of the army.

Each battle has different outcomes. The defense is victorious when no points are scored. The offense is victorious when they get a touchdown and an extra point or two-point conversion. The offense is less victorious when it scores a field goal. The back and forth of the two teams happen on a greater scale in most countries' histories. Each faction gaining the upper hand and losing it and gaining it back.

In football, those victorious in the war have the most points at the end of the game, but there will be another war next week or next season. Even after the Super Bowl, the teams will be gearing up for another test of wills and strength in a few short months.

While the metaphor in football is clear, the metaphors in baseball and softball are less so. It is easy to see what a team on the football field is trying to accomplish and why – the need for expansion and to defend home field against incursions is something that people have been doing in more or less violent forms since humans formed tribes.

Baseball and Softball

Baseball and softball have the same goal: score runs by getting on base and returning from whence you started. While football with its smashing actions and relatively high scores may be more exciting, baseball and softball may be more closely related to mundane life.

The two games are both team games and individual games. The physical play starts with a pitcher facing down a batter. The batter stands alone, and while the pitcher has a team behind him or her, the pitch itself is a lonely endeavor as the player stands on a mound exposing his or her skill to the world.

Once the pitch is made, the batter fails and gets a strike, the pitcher fails and throws a ball, or the batter succeeds and hits the ball. The batter who reacts to the pitcher gets three opportunities to fail before being called out. The pitcher, who is acting, gets four chances at failure. In life, fortune favors the bold – those who act tend to get more opportunities than those who react.

The batter can succeed with a walk, a hit, by getting hit by a pitch or with a pass ball. A walk seems like the easiest way to get on base, but it is the one that requires the best judgment and the most patience. It would be nice if walking were really that easy, but often times, the batter must hit foul tip after foul tip to get the pitcher to throw a bad one.

A hit by pitch is the most painful way to get on base. Usually the result of a mistake on the pitcher's part, getting hit never feels good even if it is one way to accomplish the goal of getting on base. A pass ball could be the fault of the pitcher or catcher, but it is the batter who gains when a called strike is not caught by the catcher.

The hit is the most exciting play of the four plays. If the batter hits the ball, he or she could still get out if the ball is caught before it touches the ground or if a defensive player gets the ball to first before the batter gets there.

While a walk is as good as a single, fans and players often focus on getting hits over getting on base. There is a sense of anticipation and mystery that comes with a hit. When the ball is put into play, there are many possibilities, and that means that chance for greater success is high. With a walk, people know what is going to happen. There is no sense of drama or possibility.

The end goal is for the player to run around the bases and get back home. Going home again is something that all men try for one reason or another. In baseball and softball, it is a literal return home, but the two sports also speak to the futility of life. After all of the effort is expended, the players have gone in a circle only to find themselves returned to where they started – even if that return is triumphant.

Maybe what is important in life is the trip away from home and the triumphant return. Everyone wants to go back to his or her high school reunion a success, but the only way to accomplish that is to explore and journey, and that journey may have to be made multiple times in order for a team to have success.

Be Active: This article came from watching my nieces play softball and my nephew play football. Take a pastime you enjoy, or have watched/participated in a lot for some reason and figure out how it relates to life. Share (#penguinate).

C: Donate! Don't Designate!

As Hurricane Irma bears down on Florida and Hurricane Jose sits in the Atlantic, they provide us with the perfect example of why you should never designate your donations. A lot of people feel better when they give to a specific disaster, so they give in the name of that disaster. The problem is that any charity worth its salt will honor those designations.

Every donation given in the name of Hurricane Harvey will be used for that hurricane and no other. Unless you are made of money (and there are only 8 people in the world who are), you will need to donate again and again as these hurricanes roll into the East Coast. It also means that those affected by fires on the West Coast aren't getting any funding and neither is anyone in Mexico or anyone affected by any other disaster.

Even if the disaster receives more donations than are needed to cover the victims, those donations are earmarked for that disaster. They cannot be used for any other disaster. Your best move is to just give to your favorite charity and let them sort out how the money is used.

The American Red Cross is on the front lines of every disaster because of its unfunded Congressional Mandate. According to Charity Navigator, approximately 90% of every dollar donated is used to help people who are covered under the mission of the Red Cross. Whether they need to pay for the electricity for their local office, they are responding to a single-family house fire, or they are sending in relief and volunteers to deal with the aftermath of a larger disaster, your best move as a donor is to give the money to your local office and let them use it as they see best. Don't let your local Red Cross suffer in the wake of a national emergency. They will be responding anyway.

If you have done your research and you are happy with the charity organization you have chosen to receive your money, they, too, should be worthy of receiving your donation without you having to designate where the funds go. Always give your money freely, and your charity organization will always be able to respond to what you want them to. Designate your funds, and your charity may not survive through the next hurricane season, even if it has plenty of earmarked money in the bank.

Be Active: I worked at the American Red Cross and saw what too many donations for one disaster did for all the other disasters that weren't as famous. Find a charity that you feel comfortable with donating to. Research the way it uses its money and donate time or money to the charity. Share (#penguinate).

Ch 12: Tell Your Story

Everyone has a story to tell, and it is a story only that person can tell. You have a story to tell. Only you can tell it. The world needs your story. It needs your creativity. Whatever medium or media you choose to tell the story in tell it. Tell it again and again. Even if you think no one is listen, reading, or looking, tell your story. It's why you're here. Remember, a story can be told with words, with pictures, through dance, through sculpture, and through your other creative endeavors.

A: Why We Need Stories

Stories help us navigate the world. They allow us to learn empathy, and they give us a different perspective on life. The right story will speak to us for whatever reason, and even if it is fiction, we will be able to see the truth within. Good stories challenge us to be better, allow us to laugh at ourselves and help us keep our humanity in a world gone insane with greed, hate, fear and stupidity. Stories can help give us a break from the never-ending impingement on our lives of the not-so-smart phones. Stories can change us and the world we live in. However, they can only do so if we allow them to be told.

Every story that is taken from us because the author or artist doesn't have enough time or energy to create is a tragic loss for the human race. People can only advance through the written word and creation of the beautiful. Many writers and artists have more than one job. The other jobs may be uplifting and provide fodder for the next story or creation, or they may be dead end, emotionally draining, creativity sinkholes that drag the creator down to the point of depression and inability to make anything new.

Even if the story and the urge to create is strong enough to get the artist to wake up at 5 am just to get it written without kids, work or the constant influx of texts, emails and virtual messengers interrupting the flow of the process, there are other things that can stop a writer from being able to produce work. A previously published writer may have difficulty getting another writing contract. She may have written book after book and know that she is good enough to be published and yet, for some unknown vagaries of the publishing system, she may not be able to get her books published. Success can be just as paralyzing as failure because success tells you can even when you aren't.

Some writers may take other writing jobs to pay the bills or to justify their existence in a capitalist society. Of course, the writing jobs that pay the best require the least amount of work, but also offer the least creative prospects, and every writer only has so many words in him per day until there is no good way to continue writing. These writers no longer write their own stories, but in the best-case scenario, they write the stories of others, and in worst-case scenarios, they write not for people but for the Internet and its algorithms so that other content can be found and its products purchased.

Writers are artists; they have their moods. When the writing muse hits and they enter the flow, the last thing they want to do is stop for any reason. Practiced writers know how to enter the flow state, but research has shown that it takes about 20 minutes of activity before the creative juices can flow at full power. (Again, it differs from person to person, but this is an average.) Depending on temperament, a writer may not want to get into a subject for fear of not having enough time to complete it.

Be Active: Whatever the reason for not creating acknowledge it, recognize its power and then dump it. Start working on your next project or continue on the project you've already started.

B: The Seven Virtues of the Samurai Writer

The world doesn't need warriors steeped in the tradition of violence and death. While Hollywood and nation-states glorify violence, murder and economic servitude, humankind cries out for a different kind of warrior – one who will uphold the traditions of the idealized, honorable warriors of the past.

These warriors may come from many different backgrounds and work in different areas; that will only make them stronger. As diverse people come together, they will be able to realize the strength that comes from cooperation.

The Samurai Writer code includes:

- Benevolence – Being good, engaging in charity, working for a better world for people.
- Courage – Having the ability to stand up for yourself and others. Speak out in the face of the crowd.
- Honesty – Be truthful with your words and actions.
- Honor – Earn the respect of others and be worthy of honor.
- Loyalty – Be faithful and devoted to the Earth, to your family, to your friends and to your cause.
- Respect – Act with courtesy. Do not be goaded by those who disbelieve or attempt to pull you in with emotions of anger and fear.
- Rectitude – Make the right decision every time, especially when it is difficult. Love is always the right choice.

Be Active: Become an intellectual warrior for the betterment of those around you and the Earth that we live on. The battle is no longer physical; it is mental and spiritual. Find your equals, partner up and do good things. Let the code of the Samurai Writer guide you.

C: What Makes for a Good Story: Revelation of Truth

There is more truth in fiction than nonfiction. Star Trek was able to have the first interracial kiss on television because it was science fiction and set in the future. Rod Serling wrote the Twilight Zone because the scripts that he wanted to write about racism and inequalities would never be accepted by Hollywood at the time. Serling used science fiction to explore social issues that would otherwise be taboo, uncomfortable or face retribution from sponsors.

Reality is a shared truth, and that means that people have to be considered when writing nonfiction. Biographies leave out inconvenient truths. Autobiographies are reconstructions rather than recalls of what happened, and even the most honest person is wary of burning bridges when writing about events that have happened, especially when the people involved are still alive.

Writers during the slave era in the South knew slavery was wrong. Yet, they continued to write in support of it because of cultural and social conventions that required them to do so to be safe both physically and in the identity that they held as Southerners.

In fiction, there are no real restrictions on the revelation of truth, except that it must, at times, be masked. A story that can reveal truth about human nature or question the current status quo while appearing at the same time innocuous and to be ridiculing those who abuse their power makes for a powerful agent of change.

Part of the reason for that is people are storytellers. People understand the language of a story better than they understand statistics and numbers larger than 20. The news relies on this for its stories. It's the reason why Fox News found the one guy who bought lobster with his food stamps and used him for several hours of interviews. Even though the actual abuse of food stamps is rare, this one story became more importance than the actual statistics.

It's the reason why stories about breast cancer aren't written with just statistics but with a celebrity's mom or someone in the community who is going through it. Though these stories aren't fiction, they also aren't the reality of the situation. They present one story, but that story is more powerful than all of the numbers and reports generated by the academic and scientific community.

Fiction runs in the same vein, but it can expose even the darkest corners of life to the light. It is in that light that people can begin to move to a better tomorrow. They just have to hear the story.

Be Active: Tell the truth. Don't echo what others around you say or believe. Think deeply about what you believe. Find that place in your heart that speaks the truth and tell that truth. It should be hard. It should be challenging. Find the place where your deepest convictions lay and then challenge those convictions, especially if you've never thought about them before. Share them #penguinate.

D: Penguins in the Pipes: The Penguin Storyteller

Barnabus and the penguins were sitting around the glowing boiler. A long night of work had just ended, and the penguins were ready to bed down for the day. However, before they went to bed, they waited for Barnabus to tell them a story.

"C'mon, dad," Lucky yawned. "I'm tired. Tell us a story."

Barnabus hugged Lucky, "Okay, daughter. Tonight, I'll tell you the Story of the Storyteller." Barnabus clicked his beak as was his custom before telling a story. Then in a beautiful tenor tone with bass undertones and the light from the flames of the boiler reflecting orange and yellow off his beak, he began:

A long time ago, before humans even evolved, there were penguins. Now, I'm not telling you anything you don't already know since you have heard tales from the past before, my little penguins. However, tonight, I am going to tell you about one of our most important figures from the past. Some might even say the most important...

Penguins don't write. It's not that we don't know how. It's not that we can't. It's just that it is extremely difficult. Grasping a writing instrument in our wings is very hard, and using our beaks to write can cause them to become dull. So, while many human cultures have preserved their history through writing. Penguins have had to keep history alive through stories. It's one of the reasons I tell you a story every morning just before bed. It keeps our history and culture alive and helps you to remember more than you realize. There is magic in storytelling; there is magic in words.

Obadiah always wore colorful clothes. That isn't to say that clothes make the penguin. It's just to point out that he was a little eccentric. Penguins don't need clothes now, and they didn't need them way back when. It's true that some penguins like to dress up, and that's okay. But Obadiah had a special reason for wearing the clothes he wore.

He had a top hat that was more patches than hat. Each patch a different color, it perfectly matched his cloak, which was so colorful, the stories say, it hurt to look at in the daytime. It certainly stood out against the snow-covered landscape of yesteryear. Obadiah would go from rookery to rookery. Keeping all penguins connected and helping everyone remember their history – if you don't know where you come from, you can't know where you are going.

Obadiah's stories were magical as were his words. Penguins would gather around to hear him perform. But I could never do

Obadiah justice, so this story isn't about the stories he told and how he told them. Instead, it is the story of how he saved all penguins from being wiped off the face of the planet.

Penguins, by nature, were never really creatures that enjoyed staying in one place. We liked to migrate – just like all the other birds. We just couldn't fly. So, we walked North or South or East or West – always in our rookeries. This brought us into other penguin rookeries. It allowed us to keep our bloodlines diverse.

Obadiah had traveled to one of the farthest North enclaves and found a group of penguins who could no longer be called a rookery. They were scared and far too few in number. Their leader had died, and only the young were left. They clamored around Obadiah and looked to him for help.

Obadiah told them a story to help calm them, and then he went to find the creature that had devastated the rookery. He knew that other penguins were coming north, and he needed to assess the threat and mitigate it if possible. Obadiah took the eldest of the penguins with him and told the others to wait for them.

The two penguins went a little farther north. The younger penguin pointed to a place just beyond the icy ridge. They snuck to the top. Obadiah removed his hat and peered over the ridge. There he saw one of the largest animals he had ever seen. It was white like the landscape, and it was feasting on a bloody carcass. A shiver ran down Obadiah's spine and not because he was cold. He rolled back behind the hill and took a deep breath.

Obadiah let out a sigh. It would probably be best to wait for that bear... It was the closest word he had for the creature... to stop eating. The only chance the penguins had to survive against that thing was to be where it wasn't. That meant negotiating a treaty. He just hoped that they were all bound together through some sort of governing group or person.

He looked over the ridge again. The bear was sitting in the snow looking bloated and sleepy. Now was the time... He nipped over the ridge leaving his companion to watch and recount the story and warn the others if Obadiah failed.

Obadiah slid down the hill and came to rest in front of the bear. He got up slowly and stood at his full height. "Hello! I'm Obadiah." He said in his friendliest voice, one that conveyed the beginning of a story.

The bear looked at him dumbly and stood up on its hind legs. Obadiah was small in comparison, very small. The bear roared down at the Obadiah – a roar that ended in a burp. The smell washed over Obadiah, and he turned slightly green.

"Hello!" Obadiah said again. "Can we talk?"

The bear dropped onto all fours. The ground shook. It sat down on its haunches and picked its teeth with its front claws. The teeth and the claws were huge. "HMMMMM," the bear grunted, "I guess so. I've just eaten, so even a little morsel like you would be too much. Let's talk. It'll give me time to digest..."

"So, right, yes," Obadiah was thinking this was a terrible plan, but it was all he had. "Like I said, I am Obadiah, and I'm a storyteller! Would you like to hear a story?"

"Alright," the bear rumbled. "I'll most likely eat you afterwards."

"Yes, fair enough." Obadiah didn't really think it was fair, but he trusted his words. "Let's begin." Obadiah twirled in his coat. The shimmering colors focused the bear's gaze on the storyteller. "Not so long ago..."

While I can't do the story justice, I can tell you that it was about a giant that ate the little animals of the world. One day, the giant ran into a group of creatures it had never seen, but since they were tiny, the giant popped them into his mouth, chewed a little and swallowed them down. The giant didn't catch them all. Those that escaped cowered in fear and waited for the giant to find them.

Fortunately for the little animals, a champion arrived, went to the giant and with his words won a boon. The giant said he would show mercy and the rest of the little creatures could go. If the creatures ever returned to the giant's territory, however, they would be fair game.

The little creatures agreed, and they never saw the giant again.

The story was so well told that the bear had tears in its eyes when it was over. While the bear may have looked dumb, he understood what Obadiah was saying, and like the giant he showed mercy to what was left of the rookery. Striking the same deal, he and his kind would stay to the North. The penguins were free to go to the South.

"That is why we and the polar bears have never lived in the same place," said Barnabus. "For with their voracious appetites and endless wanderings, the polar bears would have surely eaten every last one of us.

Of course, we penguins are facing the same fate that the penguins of yore faced. This time it comes from a far less reasonable entity – one that neither cares for species nor for life itself. It cannot care for it has no heart, and we, my little penguins, are almost powerless to stop it. But perhaps, if one of you is able to become like Obadiah, you could save the penguins and all life on Earth with one of your stories."

With the warning and a bit of hope, Barnabus sent everyone to bed. The penguins all hid for the sun was just about to rise, and they had another night of work to look forward to.

Be Active: If a penguin can be a storyteller, you can be a storyteller. Tell a story in your medium and share with #penguinate.

E: The Strongest Stories Are about Love

When Rita Vrataski, played by Emily Blunt in "Edge of Tomorrow," asks Tom Cruise's William Cage what is so special about her, in the context that he should care about saving her life over saving the Earth, Cruise has no lines. However, with his body language, silence and communication with his eyes, it is clear that Cage loves Vrataski, and that love is worth fighting for.

While "Edge of Tomorrow" wasn't a blockbuster, it also isn't terrible. Aside from Cage's amazing persistence, this sentiment may be the best thing that comes out of it. It follows the idea that Shailene Woodley's Hazel Grace tries to explain to Ansel Elgort's Augustus Waters ("The Fault in Our Stars"). Loving one person deeply should be enough. No one should have to have the superficial love of the world. In the end, it is these types of relationships – the ones about who we love – that make for the best stories.

The loving relationship doesn't have to be lovers. It can be the relationship of sisters and snowmen ("Frozen"). It can be the relationship between adopted mothers and daughters ("Maleficent"). It can be the relationship between friends as they fight the bad guys ("The Harry Potter Series," "Lord of the Rings," "Captain America: The Winter Soldier").

Maybe, that's why "Edge of Tomorrow" isn't as strong as it should be. The story doesn't focus on the relationship between Cage and Vrataski. Instead, it focuses on solving the problem of a dominant alien species destroying the planet. The relationship is a side note made of unsaid words, Cruise's acting and a final scene.

In the end, people strive to be loved and to belong. It is the stories about these strivings that make movies worth watching and books worth reading. It is these types of stories – the ones where true love always wins – that we should want more of in life and in our media.

Be Active: Write the type of story you want to read more of. Create the type of art that you want to experience more of. Be the type of creative that you think there should be more of. Share it #penguinate.

Ch 13: Find Your Support Group

I went down to my car a little after noon. I had cleaned off yesterday's snow accumulation in the morning, so I was able to just get in. As I sat in the driver's side, I noticed that there had been a few flakes that had fallen while I was in the house. They sat on my windshield beautiful in their perfection, surprising in their unexpected clarity. The fact that I could clearly see their complex structures without a microscope or magnifying glass reminded me of the wonder that we can experience in this life if we just open our eyes to see what is around us.

As I started the car, the windshield wipers wiped away the individual snowflakes, but some of the flakes squished together and held their place in spite of the efforts of the wiper. In their conglomerated state, the individuals were still visible within the whole. Parts had been melded together, but parts had kept their own form.

Those flakes, both as individuals and as a group, depended on each other for their survival. Alone, they would have been wiped away. Together they were able to avoid their own destruction, but they could only do so depending on each other.

Be Active: Find Your Support Group. Online or in the real world, whatever it takes, find people who support your work and bring you feelings of joy. Share your gratitude (#penguinate).

A: Nurture the Spark

There are stories that we like to tell ourselves so that we can cope with the machinations of a universe that does not care about us as individuals or as a species. These stories make that knowledge far more bearable than the alternative – that our little spark of light does little more than provide illumination before it is ultimately snuffed out, preferably by a short but natural lifespan, but sometimes because of other circumstances. Learned helplessness, futility and the inability to achieve a desired result in life can all lead to the dying of the flame that we must all have in order to truly burn with life.

You have met those people who have had their light snuffed out before they have actually left this plane of existence. They are the ones who do their jobs by rote and do not aspire to be anything more than they are. They may be happy in their acceptance of this life, or they may be apathetic sitting day after day in front of a media that confirms the worst of their fears without them actually realizing it. The luckiest ones have learned to compartmentalize their spark, so that it stays out when they leave their family life and comes back on when they get home. The unluckiest have no home to go to.

Our job as human beings is to keep that spark alive in ourselves and in each other as much as possible. We need to fan the flames of those passions that are a credit to the person who has them and that bring others happiness without harm. We need to find new ways to create and nurture and love, and when we see someone who may be struggling just a bit, we need to extend a hand with the milk of human kindness.

We can and should mourn every time a spark is snuffed out whether prematurely in a person who can no longer continue the fight, and yet, is too reticent to end life or in the loss of someone taken from us too soon. It is always too soon. However, we should never put ourselves in a position to regret what we could have done or should have said. Instead, we need to remember to bring to light and expound on each other's best qualities, to leave only those sings unsaid which would bring needless pain and discomfort, and to cherish the relationships that we form as we move through this world.

Life is hard enough without human beings trying to make it more difficult. We can choose to be kind. We can choose to lift each other up. We can choose to be the good in humanity. The only real problem is that we have to make the choice. Until we are able to choose better over baser, we will continue to see people lose their spark, and that hurts the world for that spark may have been the one that inspired humankind to transcend its own smallness in the universe.

Be Active: Nurture someone's creative spark, even if it's your own.

B: Creative Collaboration

Walter Isaacson's "the Innovators" is an encyclopedic recount of the invention of the modern-day computer. From Ava Lovelace to Bill Gates and Steve Jobs. Isaacson goes into depth about the eras of computer development and how analog was beat by digital. He doesn't skimp on controversies, including the different accounts of Lovelace's contributions and whether or not information should be free.

The most useful parts of the book come with the exploration of the creativity of the people that are involved in the development of the computer. Isaacson's own personal bias seems to be toward collaboration as the key to creativity.

"Creativity is a collaborative process (p. 479)." Isaacson uses Bell Labs as an example of collaboration and ideas coming together. "When the disparate practitioners and theoreticians came together," they found a common parlance and way to exchange information (p. 48). Isaacson also claims that the legal case of Eckert-Mauchly's patent claims shows "great innovations are usually the result of ideas that flow from a large number of sources... (a complex invention) usually comes from a collaboratively woven tapestry of creativity (p. 84)." There are other examples, and they point back to Isaacson's belief that creativity is more than a one-person show.

In Isaacson's view, creativity must lead to something. If the world doesn't accept it, or if it sits in the basement of a university and is never supported by anyone outside of the singular inventor, an invention is worthless. The fruits of creative endeavors must be shown to the public and become something beyond just an interesting idea gathering dust.

Be Active: Find someone to do a project with. Work the project to completion.

Ch 14: Inspiration from Famous Creators

You don't have to be famous to learn something from famous creators or their creations. Take your inspiration where you can get it and enjoy these tales from people who have accomplished many different creative goals.

A: Walt Disney's Road to Creativity

Walt Disney was born in Chicago, Illinois in 1901. He moved with his family to Marceline, Missouri in 1906. Walt credited Marceline with such great influence in his life that he believed nothing more influential was likely to happen to him in the future. For a five-year-old, the family farm provided opportunities to explore the natural world and be creative.

Walt was known not only for his hijinks that included using tar to draw on the family barn, but also for his skits and drawings that he would do for the local barber shop. People would pay him for his drawings and praise his creativity.

For Abraham Lincoln's birthday, Walt dressed up as the 16th president. The principal was so impressed with Walt's outfit and memorization of Lincoln's Gettysburg Address that he took Walt to all of the school's classrooms to play Lincoln for the day. It was this type of encouragement from the small town of Marceline that sent Walt on his way.

Walt once described himself as a bee. He would go from workspace to workspace and help his employees by making ideas better – kind of like pollinating flowers. He would dog ideas until they became workable and rarely forgot anything.

People would often think that Walt was distracted, but Walt's mind moved so fast that he could remember everything that happened and what people said, even when he appeared not to be paying attention.

Walt was not only dogged in his pursuit of ideas. He was implacable when it came to confronting naysayers and barriers. He did not let lack of money stop him. Fortunately, he was able to share power with his brother Roy, who was able to provide the financial expertise that Walt may have lacked. It was through this partnership that Walt and Roy were able to build the Disney Empire.

Walt had several obstacles that he had to overcome. His company Laugh-O-Grams failed, and he moved out to Hollywood with $40 in his pocket and a reel of the Alice comedies. People doubted Walt Disney more than they supported him with both the first animated feature film, "Snow White and the Seven Dwarfs" called Disney's folly, and Disneyland. The eternal optimist, Walt knew when he was right and went ahead.

While Walt accomplished many things in his life including Mickey Mouse, "Snow White and the Seven Dwarfs," the forerunner to stereo, and Disneyland, what he would be most proud of is creating an organization that continues to provide happiness and innovation. Walt was a man whose undying enthusiasm has its expression in the Walt Disney Company. Happiness is truly what Walt wanted to bring to people.

Walt believed that "the way to get started is to quit talking and begin doing." While many people believe that creativity comes from long periods of introspection and quick inspiration, it is more often provided in the action of doing things aimed toward a goal that is larger than one can reasonably expect to reach.

Be Active: Quit reading and start doing! Grab your next creative project and work on it. Don't know what it is, yet? Brainstorm and start a new project. Share with "#penguinate."

B: Rod Serling and the Fifth Dimension

Your favorite plot twist in a movie or on television probably owes its existence to one show, The Twilight Zone, and that show's creator, Rod Serling. Because Serling wanted to deal with the big issues of the day, but censorship and sponsorships conspired against his shows set in the modern day, he turned to science fiction as a way to make his statements against war and racism while exploring man's nature and humankind's inexhaustible need to hate someone else.

When Serling attempted to tell the story of Emmett Till, a young black man that was lynched in the American South for whistling at a white woman and for which the men who had killed him were acquitted, the network and the sponsors set the story in the Northeast and "chopped it up like a roomful of butchers at work on a steer" (Lacy, 1995) making Serling's story irrelevant.

As the most decorated television writer of his time with three Emmy awards before The Twilight Zone debuted, Serling commanded the respect of his peers and the power to combat the censors and sponsors. However, acting the "role of a tired non-conformist" (Wallace, 1959), he looked to The Twilight Zone as a way to continue writing without having to worry so much about what the network would try to do with his work.

In an interview with Mike Wallace (1959), Serling said that his new series could not deal with social criticism because they were too short. "These are strictly for entertainment," said Serling. "Because they deal in the areas of fantasy and imagination and science fiction and all of those things, there's no opportunity to cop a plea or chop an axe or anything... I'm not going to try to delve into current social problems dramatically."

While looking at the themes of The Twilight Zone including racism and the horrors of war, this statement may seem disingenuous. Science fiction had been used by Ray Bradbury to make social commentary with the 1953 release of Fahrenheit 451 and both Jules Verne and H. G. Wells in earlier works. However, for Serling, drama has a very specific meaning that encompasses his earlier works. Requiem for a Heavyweight, Patterns and The Comedian, his award-winning dramas, were set in present day and thus dramatically presented social issues. Science fiction and fantasy did not have the same gravitas and could escape the censors as something not to be taken seriously.

According to writer Richard Matheson, "he [Serling] carried his Playhouse 90 sensibility right into the The Twilight Zone and found that stories of social commentary that you could not sell anywhere under any other circumstances but you put it in a fantasy story and you could say all sorts of things" (Lacy, 1995). Indeed, Serling himself commented that he "found that it was all right to have Martians saying things Democrats and Republicans could never say" (PBS, 2003).

Nature vs. Nurture

According to David Bell's presentation of Donna Haraway's Cyborg Manifesto (2006), most either/or questions are false dichotomies that could be rephrased as neither/both. The idea that it is nature versus nurture is a neat dichotomy that would make life simpler if people could lay the cause of complex human behavior in the genes or upbringing and experience of a person. However, it takes a combination of nature and nurture to help make someone creative. This is supported by Hughson and Hughson (2004), who state that no one really believes that nature versus nurture (or heredity versus environment) is a "real dichotomy" and "that both contribute."

According to Csikszentmihalyi (2013), "genetic predisposition for a specific domain" (p. 52) may help with creativity, but there are examples of creators who lacked the genetics, like Beethoven who couldn't hear "when he composed his greatest works" and El Greco who had an optic disease, to account for their creativity. Csikszentmihalyi believes that the predisposition may lead to an interest in a domain, but it takes access to that domain in order to realize the creativity therein.

Serling's father was a grocer, who ran his own store. This shows a certain capability in entrepreneurship, which is related to creativity. However, it is not directly related to the art of writing. While this may have had some influence, World War II and the death of his father had greater influences. Serling went through World War II as a paratrooper and came out a changed man. "I was traumatized into writing by war events. By going through a war in a combat situation and feeling the desperate need for some sort of therapy. Get it out of my gut; write it down. This is the way it began for me" (Lacy, 1995).

The Creative Personality

According to Csikszentmihalyi (2013), creative people have personalities that embrace ten antithetical traits. While any individual creative person may not have all ten traits, it is common for the creator to exhibit traits that others would find confusing. Paradoxically, creative people are energetic some times and completely still during other times. They are imaginative and rooted in reality. They are rebellious and conservative.

"Creative individuals have a great deal of physical energy, but they are also often quiet and at rest" (Csikszentmihalyi, 2013, p. 58). During the run of The Twilight Zone, Serling worked 12-hour days, seven days a week. Even when he would go to his vacation home in Ithaca, he would still be working. By the fourth season of The Twilight Zone, he said, "I'm writing faster now than ever before... It's the kind of schedule that if I drop a pencil and then bend over to pick it up, I am two weeks behind" (Lacy, 1995). According to producer Bert Granet, "he wrote continuously; he worked continuously. I just think he had been a motor that had been running so fast so long" (Lacy, 1995).

Serling knew that he needed a break. "I've never felt quite so drained of ideas as I do at this moment. Stories used to bubble out of me so fast that I couldn't set them down on paper quick enough. But in the last few years, I've written so much I'm woozy. If only I could take off about six months and replenish the well" (Lacy, 1995).

"It's been a rough time professionally and personally. And the prospect of the cool lake, the boat and the beautifully run-down cottage seems infinitely desirable" (Lacy, 1995).

"Rod used Ithaca as a personal retreat," said Mike Wallace (Lacy, 1995).

"Creative individuals alternate between imagination and fantasy at one end, and a rooted sense of reality at the other" (Csikszentmihalyi, 2013, p. 63). Serling was the most decorated writer of a young television era with his three Emmy wins for stories that were decidedly contemporary.

Unfortunately, the networks and the advertisers did not like the fact that Serling wanted to explore social issues like racism and prejudice. When Serling submitted a story about Emmett Till, a young black man who was lynched in the South for having the temerity to whistle at a white woman and whose lynchers, including the sheriff of the town, were acquitted at trial, the networks moved the location from the South to New England and went so far as to remove Coca Cola bottles from the set because they were to representative of the South.

Serling knew that he couldn't continue to battle the networks and sponsors in a contemporary world. He turned to science fiction and fantasy and created the Twilight Zone, which he told Mike Wallace in an interview would have no social criticism. The shows would be too short and "deal in the areas of fantasy and imagination..." He also said that he had given up in delving into current social problems.

Rooted in the reality of the TV landscape, Serling found a way to navigate the mines of censorship. That meant delving into his imagination for the fantastical stories that influenced future generations and are still relevant today. An alien on TV can say what a Republican or Democrat cannot.

"Generally, creative people are thought to be rebellious and independent... Yet it is impossible to be creative without having first internalized a domain of culture... hence, he or she must be to a certain extent a traditionalist" (Csikszentmihalyi, 2013, p. 71). Serling found himself in a relatively young profession of television script writing, which meant that there were fewer traditions to follow as far as writing was concerned. However, there was still a system of censors and sponsors. Serling rebelled against the system by creating a form of television that would allow him to get his messages of social responsibility to the audience while stymieing the efforts of the censors and sponsors. He realized that he was dealing with people who were not necessarily intelligent enough to see the big picture, especially when they were worried about minutia like Coca Cola bottles on the set as being too Southern.

Yet, he also took jobs that he knew he wouldn't like because he needed the money, and he succumbed to the fame that Hollywood gave him. While he originally got out of writing advertisements because it was "a particularly dreamless occupation" (Wallace, 1959), he still became a spokesperson for other products like cigarettes and beer. "It must have been devastating for him, devastating, because it was against everything he stood for all through his career," said Wallace (Lacy, 1995).

"My crime has been committed, and there is very little defense for it. I was not conned into doing the beer commercial. Rather a sizable check was thrust in front of me, and I plowed in with no thought as to its effect or ramifications" (Lacy, 1995). This allowed him to feed his family and keep his income at an acceptable level for his lifestyle, but it also diminished his idealism.

Intrinsic Vs. Extrinsic Motivation

According to Amabile and Kramer (2011), "intrinsic motivation is the love of the work itself – doing the work because it is interesting, enjoyable, satisfying, engaging, or personally challenging" (p. 34).

Serling had the internal drive of an artist with his internal motivation coming from his experiences with death in WWII and his father. He said he succumbed to writing, and he had a desire to take on the issues of his time, including prejudice (Lacy, 1995). This internal motivation was enough to get him out of the lucrative but soulless job of advertising and testimonial writing and into writing scripts for television (Wallace, 1959). His first scripts would take him six months to a year to complete with no guarantee that they would be accepted by any of the networks.

Amabile and Kramer (2011) say that extrinsic motivation is "the motivation to do something in order to get something else" (p. 34). Once the system dragged him in, like the main character in Serling's 'The Velvet Alley,' which was termed autobiographical (Lacy, 1995), money became a driving motivator. He did commercials and ended his career with The Night Gallery, a show on which he had no creative control. He wrote the scripts, and the network changed them as it saw fit. Yet, Serling's name was tied to the show.

"He was such a dichotomy; he was an enigma. He wanted success, he wanted money, he wanted celebrity status, he wanted to be a star, and yet, underneath it was this terribly honest, very gifted artist, and I don't think he could ever reconcile the two driving forces of his psyche," said director John Frankenheimer.

Serling died on the surgeon's table suffering from a heart attack at the age of 50 in 1975. He was undergoing what was then a cutting-edge procedure. During his life, he had accumulated six Emmys and left behind a legacy of influence on science fiction writers, nightmares for television viewers and a television series that lasted longer than anyone would have imagined. More importantly, he left behind a family who was able to experience him as a loving father in spite of the long hours that he worked.

Be Active: What movie or show twist surprised you? Share with #penguinate and #spoilers. Better, try to share it while still being spoiler-free!

References

Amabile, T., & Kramer, S. (2011). The progress principle: Using small wins to ignite joy, engagement, and creativity at work. Harvard Business Press.

Bell, D. (2006). Cyberculture Theorists: Manuel Castells and Donna Haraway. Routledge.

Csikszentmihalyi, M. (2013). Creativity: The Psychology of Discovery and Invention (Harper Perennial Modern Classics ed.). U.S.A.: HarperCollins.

Gunn, J. (1970). Science Fiction in Literature

Hughson, N., & Hughson, R. (2004). Psychology of Creativity. (pp. Ch 6). Arizona: Amazing Books.

Lacy, S. (Producer), & Lacy, S. (Director). (1995). Rod Serling: Submitted for Your Approval. [Video/DVD] CBS Entertainment Production.

PBS. (2003). Rod Serling: About Rod Serling. Retrieved from http://www.pbs.org/wnet/americanmasters/episodes/rod-serling/about-rod-serling/702/

Rod Serling. (2015). The Biography.com website. Retrieved 10:36, May 27, 2015, from http://www.biography.com/people/rod-serling-9479196.

Wallace, M. (1959). The Mike Wallace Interview with Rod Serling.

C: Elizabeth Gilbert on Creativity and Suffering

In her "Your elusive creative genius" TED talk, Elizabeth Gilbert, author of "Eat, Pray, Love," addresses the idea that "creativity and suffering are inherently linked." With the narrative that so many creative people have died because of their works, Gilbert finds the idea a bit off-putting, especially since she is so young, and it is likely that her greatest success has already happened.

Norman Mailer said that "every one of my books has killed me a little more." Gilbert argues that it doesn't have to be that way. If artists and society can accept the idea that people are not necessarily genius, but experience moments of genius, it would help relieve the pressure that has been killing off the artists of the Western World. Gilbert believes that it would be better to encourage the world's creative minds to live; rather than allow them to be taken from the planet early in their lives.

Artists do what they do because they love to do it, it is a calling, but it is also a job. According to Gilbert, the artist's job isn't to create something that others believe is genius but to just show up and to keep showing up. If something comes of it that is genius, then great. If not, at least the artist has done his or her job.

Artists and creative people need to support each other. When those who are creative come together to lift each other up, they will create a more conducive atmosphere to better creativity and a nurturing place where failure is encouraged and people can feel safe in their own creative processes.

Be Active: Watch Elizabeth Gilbert's talk and then find your support group or make one. Get help nurturing your creativity.

D: Community Based Storytelling with 'Blood and Gourd'

D.H. Shultis, co-creator and co-writer of the "Blood & Gourd," sees the corporate culture as one that may imperil community-based storytelling because corporations that tell most of the stories today are only looking at stories that will make money. These profitable stories can be limited in scope and just plain boring because they are all the same story.

"It's just human to tell stories," says Shultis.

Shultis sees the independent market as a continuation of what people have done throughout history: tell stories around the campfire, within the oral tradition, books and other media.

"It's really about getting stories out there that matter," says Shultis.

"Blood & Gourd" is about pumpkins taking over Olympia, WA, where he and co-creator Jenz K. Lund went to grad school.

"We decided to write where we know," says Shultis, who is based in Portland along with the publishing company Dead Peasant. "On the surface, it's a really simple horror story."

However, Shultis also says that the story is fun, and it is "about doing the thing that needs to be done even if you don't want to do it."

While Shultis is a licensed counselor, he feels a burning need to create every day, and "Blood & Gourd" is part of the fruits of his labor. The excitement he feels about the book comes from the creative process.

"This is what our life can be about," says Shultis. "Get out there and create."

Be Active: Find another independent artist or writer and support them as best you can. Share that support (#penguinate).

E: Songwriter Steve Dorff on Song Writing

"It's a blessed life. You get to do what you love to do. It's hard work," says Steve Dorff. "It's filled with rejection every day at every single level."

Songwriters need to hustle if they want to be successful.

"I have always operated by the principle 'whatever it takes,'" says Dorff. "If you get to meet the bus driver that's driving George Strait's bus" do whatever you can to get the demo into the star's hands. "If you can self-publish it, that's great," but you do anything you can to get that music out there.

Meeting other people will help a writer be successful and find someone else to work with.

"There's no substitute for networking," says Dorff. "Most of the great songs come from great collaborators."

Songs are stories in and of themselves, and songwriters need to know what the beginning, middle and end of the story are before writing it.

"You're coming up with this little movie in your mind," says Dorff, "and you kind of have to figure that out, or you'll be writing a long time."

Dorff spoke at Salt Lake Community College's South City Campus on March 21, 2014, as part of the Songwriter's Summit in Utah. Dorff has written for people like Willie Nelson and Whitney Houston. He also has a Broadway musical under his belt and is the "cat daddy" of all genres of music according to Dean Dillon.

BMI Vice President of Licensing Dan Spears says that Dorff is among the elite songwriters. "There are a lot of great voices out there but not a lot of great songwriters."

Be Active: Write a song. Share it (#penguinate).

F: The Last Good Day

In "The Fault in Our Stars," Hazel Grace explains the idea of The Last Good Day. For cancer sufferers, this is a day when things are going well. The bad days seem to have plateaued, and there may be a period of relative health. Then it goes downhill rather quickly.

Because death is a universal experience, everyone has a Last Good Day. Cancer patients aren't the only ones who experience death, but they do have a more intimate association with death than most other people because they actively live with its threat.

The two words that are important as far as "The Fault in Our Stars" and the previous sentence are concern are "actively live." Hazel Grace and Augustus Waters do the things they need to do to live a full life, even though they are faced with dying young. Neither one is really dying any more than anyone else, and they are doing their best job at living, which cannot be said for all healthy people.

One of the lessons from "The Fault in Our Stars" is that life is precious and valuable. It is meant to be lived in the best way possible regardless of circumstances. Being healthy is no excuse for wasting one good day, and those good days should include friends, family and learning.

When you wake up, ask yourself if this will be your Last Good Day. You won't know the answer, but if you live it right, it could be the start of several good days.

Be Active: Do something that you would do if you knew this was your last good day. Share what you did (#penguinate).

G: Everything I Needed to Know about Creativity I Learned from Matt Smith's Doctor Who

When it comes to exploration, absurdity and creativity, there is no one better than Matt Smith's Doctor Who. An explorer, Doctor Who has always found ways to defeat his enemies and save the world; however, the quirks that Smith portrays in his version of the Doctor make him a great foray into, and inspiration, for anyone who wants to become more creative.

Have a companion – One of the admonitions that Doctor Who hears from his former companions is that he needs to find someone to travel with. Amy Pond and River Song have both told him that it isn't good for him to be alone, and it isn't. By himself, Doctor Who tends to lose sight of who he is. His companion helps him remember his identity and keeps his baser self in check.

That doesn't mean that the Doctor has to have someone with him all of the time. It just means that having someone allows the Doctor to be his best self, bounce ideas off of that person and even learn important things from another.

Fezzes and bowties are cool – Doctor Who has his own sense of style. The fez has not withstood the test of time, but the bow tie remains, and he has picked up a set of reading glasses from Pond. Having a sense of style that is his own allows the Doctor to remember who he is. It also allows him to have a sense of integrity when it comes to his personality and principles. As long as he can straighten his bow tie, he can solve the next impossible problem. Having a personal sense of style allows the Doctor to declare his difference, and it allows others to accept his quirks.

Anachronism – Because the Doctor doesn't have a time or he has all of time, he is a walking anachronism. The Tardis, the Blue Police Box that is the Doctor's time machine, can be found in Ancient Egypt, in Pompeii before the volcano explodes, and in any other time. It may not always be anachronistic, but it is not always of the time that it is found in. When Queen Nefertiti visits the 1902 African Savannah with a space alien gun, there are some serious time disturbances that are going on.

Absurdity – Doctor Who doesn't always make sense when it is confronted by lateral thinking, and sometimes, it just doesn't make any sense to a rational thought process. However, what it does do is have a lot of fun with a very complex universe that it has created – 50 years of the same TV show about a man in a time machine that travels through space and time should get old. Doctor Who hasn't gotten old, even if he is 1,200 years old.

"Dinosaurs on a Spaceship" is a big example of the absurdity on Doctor Who. This absurdity leads to incredibly creative adventures that might otherwise have gone unwritten.

Characteristics – Aside from being incredibly smart and not saddled with the same worries about death, bills, or taxes, Doctor Who has several characteristics that make him creative. He takes pleasure in the simple things like fish fingers and custard, even when he doesn't like them.

He has a strong moral code, and he stands up for what he believes in regardless of the odds against him. His courage gives him the power to overcome those odds; it also gives him the power to come up with creative solutions.

He is always positive. No matter how dark things look, he has a smile and something crazy to say. The details matter to him, and it is often the simple thing that propels his plan to success. The Doctor uses all of his senses, but it isn't just that he uses all of his sense, it is that he uses them in ways that most people wouldn't even consider – he has tasted a leaf that was pasted in a book.

Explore – The whole of space and time is at your fingertips. Where do you want to go and what do you want to see? The Doctor and his companions are explorers. They want to see everything that the universe has to offer. Even better, they want to experience everything. There is significant risk in many of the trips and projects they undertake, but they do them anyway because, in the end, what they are doing is more important than the worst individual outcome that they can think of.

Smith's Doctor Who takes all of these qualities and combines them into a compassionate, loving, slightly odd man, and along with his companions, he is allowed to be the most creative man in the universe on the most creative show currently on television. A few other shows have matched the creativity of Doctor Who, but none have surpassed it.

Be Active: Put on a fez and bowtie. Share the photo with "#penguinate." Choose to explore some place else or some other time. Choose a book to help you do so. It's bigger on the inside.

Ch 15: Be Epic

According to Seth Godin, "We try to make big, important change, but we don't talk about it in that way." People want to be epic. They want to experience that feeling that they get from watching movies and vicariously living through characters on screen. People want to do something important.

It is this sense of being able to do something epic that is lacking in life today. Fear of failure, fear of making mistakes, fear of ridicule hold people back from doing what they truly want to do. As much as people want to be part of something greater than they are alone, they also want to be comfortable. The media hasn't done anyone any favors with its portrayal of how easy epic should be. Put together a three-minute training montage, and the boxer becomes the heavyweight champion of the world.

Epic just doesn't happen. Epic takes time. Ulysses' epic adventure happened over the course of a decade. He faced several challenges including his own short-term desires and sorcery before he could get back home to his wife and son.

Epic takes ability. Someone who wants to accomplish something epic will have to train in those skills necessary to accomplish the feat. The average person cannot just hop in a sailboat and sail around the world. The trip takes planning, knowledge and skill. When it happens, it will be epic, but it cannot successfully happen without having the ability to sail.

Epic takes luck. While luck might be opportunity meeting preparation, there are times when events are out of a person's control. Being prepared will give the person the best opportunity to make epic happen, but sometimes, it just takes a little luck to go just a little further. Maybe it is a gust of wind, maybe it is well-placed word of encouragement, whatever it is, it will be just enough to push the person accomplishing the epic feat over the top

Epic sometimes goes unnoticed. When Ulysses finally arrived home, he found men waiting to court his wife. Ulysses had to hide until the time was right to reveal who he was. There was no fanfare celebrating his return, just a group of power-hungry men waiting to wed his wife.

Epic requires patience. In a world where instant gratification is a thing and adult attention spans are dwindling to that of less than a goldfish, patience is hard to come by. Delayed gratification and self-satisfaction are undervalued in many cases. They are required for the epic event to truly be epic.

Be Active 1: Replace the word "epic" with "creativity" or "creative" and reread the above essay.

Be Active 2: Watch Seth Godin's TED Talk "The Tribes We Lead." Share what you learned (#penguinate).

Be Active 3: Start toward your epic incarnation. Share your goals and take your time (#penguinate).

More Inspiration

Try These Books and Authors.

Books for the Young and Young at Heart:

- Lewis Carroll: Alice in Wonderland, Through the Looking Glass.
- Roald Dahl: Anything, including Charlie and the Chocolate Factory.
- Charles Dickens: A Christmas Carol.
- Shad Engkilterra: The Adventures on the Amur series.
- John Esposito: Tales from the Haunted Mansion Vol. 1: The Fearsome Foursome.
- A.A. Milne: Winnie the Pooh stories.

Books for Teens and Above:

- K.M. Alexander: The Stars Were Right.
- Ray Bradbury: Anything, including Something Wicked This Way Comes and Fahrenheit 451.
- Bree Despain: The Dark Divine.
- Mikhail Bulgakov: Master and Margarita.
- Sir Arthur Conan Doyle: Sherlock Holmes.
- Alexandre Dumas: The Three Musketeers.
- Shad Engkilterra: The Pirate Union.
- Rachel E. Kelly: The Colorworld Series.
- Isaac Marion: Warm Bodies, The Burning World.
- Raven Oak: Amaskan's Blood.
- Veronica Roth: Divergent.
- Rod Serling: Stories from the Twilight Zone, More stories from the Twilight zone, Night Gallery.
- Kaye Thornbrugh: Flicker.
- Jules Verne: Anything, including 20,000 Leagues under the Sea.
- H.G. Wells: Anything, including The Time Machine.
- Natalie Whipple: Transparent, Blindsided.

Adult Reading:

- Brian C. Baer: Bad Publicity.
- Dashiell Hammett: The Maltese Falcon.
- Darren Lamb: The Sea of Sin series, The Book of Benjamin.
- Drue M. Scott: Quantum Souls series.

Non-fiction Reads:

- Brian C. Baer: How He-Man Mastered the Universe: Toy to Television to the Big Screen.

- Ed Catmull: Creativity, Inc.
- Felicia Day: You're Never Weird on the Internet (almost).
- Cary Elwes: As you Wish: Inconceivable Tales from the Making of The Princess Bride.
- Shad Engkilterra: My Life in the Projects: A kid's-eye view of HUD housing in the 1980s, Disneyland Is Creativity: 25 Tips for Becoming More Creative.
- Darren Lamb: Ronin Buddhism.
- Drue M. Scott: Found on the Alcan.
- Marty Sklar: Dream It! Do It!
- Aaron Wallace: The Thinking Fan's Guide to Walt Disney World: The Magic Kingdom, Hocus Pocus in Focus: The Thinking Fan's Guide to Disney's Halloween Classic.

Graphic Novels and Comics:

- Dead Peasant's Blood and Gourd
- Benjamin Kreger, Edward Ellsworth and Dexter Wee: The Black Suit of Death
- Nate Quarry: Zombie Cage Fighter
- Ron Randall: Trekker
- Greg Smith, Michael Tanner and Zach Lehner: Junior Braves of the Apocalypse
- Manny Trembley: Victoria Jr.

Check out these Movies and Series.

Documentaries:

- Atomic Mom
- Being Elmo: A Puppeteer's Journey
- Botany of Desire
- Carbon Nation
- El Bulli
- Happy
- Miss Representation

Based on Actual Events:

- Get on Up: Based on the life of James Brown.
- The Imitation Game: Based on the events of Alan Turing's life starring Benedict Cumberbatch.
- Million Dollar Arm: Bringing India to baseball.
- Money Ball: The story of statistics and baseball.

Mainstream:

- The Avengers: Marvel's superhero movie is masterful at giving every character something important to do and having them all come together.
- Big Hero 6: Creativity abounds; sometimes you just got to shake it up.
- Citizen Kane with Orson Welles: The greatest movie ever made.
- Destino: Disney, Dali and 58 years of time to bring it out.
- Fantasia: Disney's music and film masterpiece.
- Frozen: Don't let it go; it flipped Disney Princess films, or at least one naïve snowman, on their head.
- The Jazz Singer with Al Jolson: The first talkie.
- Meet the Robinsons: Creativity at the fore.
- The Muppets with Jason Segel and Amy Adams.
- One Direction: This Is Us – Having fun, see it with fans.
- Saving Mr. Banks: The fictionalized story of Walt Disney bringing Mary Poppins to the screen explores Pamela Travers relationship to the character and the book.
- Scrooge with Albert Finney: A musical version of "A Christmas Carol."
- The Secret Life of Walter Mitty with Ben Stiller.
- Snow White and the Seven Dwarfs: The first full-length animated feature.
- Tomorrowland with George Clooney: Picture creativity and the dreamers.

Foreign Films:

- Furious: The Legend of Kolovrat (Russia).
- The Last Warrior (Russia): A Disney co-production.

- The Guardians (Zashchitniki, Russia): The Russian Avengers.
- My Girlfriend Is a Gumiho (Korea): A TV show about a nine-tailed magical fox and love.

Television:

- Steven Spielberg Presents Amazing Stories (1985 – 1987): A gift from the same person who brought E.T. to life among others.
- Buffy the Vampire Slayer: What if the monsters feared the blonde cheerleader? Episodes like "Hush" and "Once More with Feeling" are classic.
- Doctor Who: Doctor's Nine through 12 were fun. I haven't seen all of the episodes with Capaldi and later.
- Netflix's Lemony Snickett's A Series of Unfortunate Events: Maybe you should skip this one; it's filled with nothing but dismay. Look away.
- The Outer Limits: Not as good as its predecessor, the Twilight Zone.
- The Ray Bradbury Theater (1985 – 1992): Another storytelling genius.
- Scorpion: A group of geniuses solve problems, but you don't have to be a genius to pick up some hints.
- The Twilight Zone (1959 – 1964): A classic exploration of the macabre and the twist ending.
- Z-Nation: Consistently a well-written and surprising show if you can get past the gore and the Asylum name.

Afterword

Thank you for joining me on this creative journey. I hope you found inspiration to improve your own creativity and to help make the world and your life better. If you liked this book, please leave a review at Amazon and wherever you may find book review opportunities. If you want to learn more about creativity and you like Disneyland, check out "Disneyland Is Creativity: 25 Tips for Becoming More Creative."

Go out and penguinate!

About the Author

Shad Engkilterra earned a Master's of Creativity and Innovation from the Edward de Bono Institute at the University of Malta. His lifelong love of Disney, including a stint in Walt Disney World's College Program where he founded a group called the Penguinators, led him to pursue the degree in an effort to find ways to help others become more creative. Jenya, Shad's wife, makes handmade penguins and took the photo for the cover of this book.